# A R T I C U L A T I O N S

# A R T I C U L A T I O N S

## The Body and Illness in Poetry

### Edited by Jon Mukand

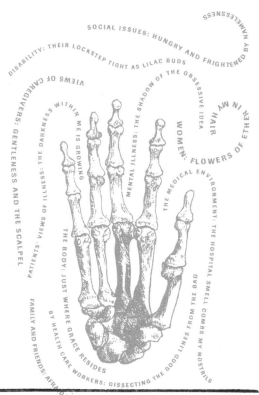

UNIVERSITY OF IOWA PRESS Ψ IOWA CITY

University of Iowa Press, Iowa City 52242
Printed in the United States of America

Design by Karen Copp

Permissions begin on page 405.

Printed on acid-free paper

Library of Congress
Cataloging-in-Publication Data
Articulations: the body and illness in poetry /
edited by Jon Mukand.
    p.    cm.
    Includes index.
    ISBN 0-87745-478-7 (pbk.)
    1. American poetry—20th century.
2. Care of the sick—Poetry.  3. Mental
illness—Poetry.  4. Mentally ill—
Poetry.  5. Body, Human—Poetry.
6. Hospitals—Poetry.  7. Diseases—Poetry.
8. Patients—Poetry.  I. Mukand, Jon,
1949–  .
PS595.C37A78  1994
811'.914080920824—dc20      94-16528
                          CIP

01  00  99  98  97  96  95  94  P  5  4  3  2  1

*for my daughter,*

*Nita Hannah*

# Contents

**Patients' Views of Illness:**
**The Darkness within Me Is Growing**

**Views of Caregivers:**
**Gentleness and the Scalpel**

## Mental Illness: The Shadow of the Obsessive Idea

## Acknowledgments

I am grateful to all the poets and publishers who have granted permission to reprint these poems. The process of compiling this anthology has been especially rewarding because of the generosity of so many people.

In recognition of its vital work, all proceeds from this book are being donated to the Stroke section of the American Heart Association.

To my wife and colleague, Giselle Corré, I am always indebted for so much.

# Introduction

The sliding doors softly glide shut, and the receptionist waits, ready to send the visitor to the correct floor, wing, and room. This person is one of the luckier ones, who didn't have to be wheeled in by the paramedics, who didn't need chest compression, oxygen, intravenous drugs, and a siren announcing the emergency to the city. Maybe the visitor is a rabbi or a priest, an impartial giver of comfort; but the patient might be someone closer, a sister or a father or a husband. This may be the first visit or the fortieth. In either case, the visitor soon learns that the hospital is a unique place: an island, an oasis, an oracle. When the border of those benign glass doors is crossed, one has entered a different culture. Only certain areas can be seen, such as the waiting rooms, patient rooms, and nursing stations; the procedure rooms—where sterility is essential, where bodies must be invaded in order to heal them, where existence is more unpredictable than usual—are restricted.

This place has its own language and the layperson must have an interpreter, which creates a sense of mystery or even secrecy. But the hospital cannot function without certain linguistic peculiarities. Phrases such as "IV Push," "No Code," and "Stat Nitro" are integral to rapid and smooth communication. Sometimes this can be quite unnerving to the patient, who must place complete trust in the hospital personnel. This "language barrier" can also be a source of some humorous mix-ups. Once an elderly patient, quite concerned about Alzheimer's Dementia, asked whether she had "Oldtimer's Disease."

The patient who has been abruptly removed to unfamiliar surroundings may experience disorientation or even disbelief at the fact of being ill. Patients in Intensive Care Units—exposed to incessant activity and various noises from respirators and intravenous pumps—are often sleep-deprived and can develop "ICU psychosis." Some have to be restrained from pulling out the intubation tube or urinary catheter. Others are in denial. Once I had to treat a young man who refused to believe he had suffered a heart attack and demanded to be discharged from the ICU because he had to give a lecture at a prestigious university!

In medicine, the inverted logic of tests causes a "positive" result to be bad (a disease is diagnosed) and a "negative" one to be good. But it is better to have a "false positive" than a "false negative," since the latter means that the diagnosis was missed! Medical tests may involve some discomfort, such as multiple needle-sticks, enemas, or fasting. The first thing an elderly woman once told me when I introduced myself as a consultant was, "I'm not having any more X-rays!" She still remembered, vividly, her last GI series.

Of all the people I have seen in the medical setting, those about to have X-rays are the most uneasy group. Clad in hospital gowns, quiet, cheerless, they are often waiting for the penetrating beams to pinpoint a diagnosis. Some conjure up all sorts of images about the procedure, especially if a CAT scan or a radiolabeled material is used for the sake of contrast. Other patients take them in stride. After carefully examining one of my patients, I said he would probably need an Indium scan. He replied, "Why? I've already had my *Indian* scan. You've poked and prodded just about every part of me!"

Patients try to understand the medical environment in different ways, through intellectualization or withdrawal or hostility, to name just a few responses. A very intelligent, middle-aged man dying of cancer expected me to know all his lab results on rounds, especially the calcium level, which was related to his nausea and vomiting. Not unexpectedly, his symptoms seemed to wax and wane with the degree of hypercalcemia *reported* to him every day. Another patient, who was an auto mechanic, was told that his lungs had crackles; he replied that they were made for only so many miles and asked me if we replaced worn-out carburetors.

The medical environment is perceived in a variety of ways by family and friends of the patient. They may also feel disoriented and may have to confront their own mortality. The husband of a woman who needed a bypass graft around an occluded artery refused to permit a pelvic operation; he was afraid she would develop cancer of the uterus as a result! When complications developed after a less optimal operation and another surgery became necessary, he insisted on a second opinion, which meant a delay. He loved his wife dearly, perhaps too well for her own good.

Even to the initiate, the hospital is mysterious. While I typed these words, the light in a room on the sixth floor, the cancer ward, went off, leaving a streetlight's fluorescent glare. Was it someone I knew? From my window, I could not tell. Maybe the patient, relaxed after a scheduled dose of morphine, floated down into sleep like a snowflake; maybe the body simply held its breath, refusing to give any more mouth-to-mouth resuscitation to this world, and sank into the depths of white linen. Tomorrow morning, I might find out what happened. But tonight, my pager is off.

While treating patients on a Spinal Cord Injury unit, I saw a spectrum of emotions ranging from profound depression to incoherent anger—in the same patient. Subtle changes also occur. For instance, in a group of patients with recent paralysis, I found that time appeared to move slowly and be stretched out in the present, the future seemed to be contracted, and the past was remote; in the final analysis, the patient was left in a sort of temporal limbo.

A patient who had recently been weaned off her heroin habit was tearfully demanding opiates, supposedly for a toothache. Her eyes were dilated, and her tone was becoming strident. Opiates have the side effect of constricting the pupils; maybe the light of this world was too bright for her. I had to place an intravenous line but couldn't find any veins. They were all used up! My attending physician, more experienced at dealing with addicts, showed me a vein in her shoulder and we managed to start a line. She was poorly cooperative, even in the hospital, and probably went back to her drugs. For her, time stood still until her next dose, or overdose.

I have encountered a spectrum of views toward a physician, from near-deification to hostility in the form of physical violence. At the one extreme, I had managed to convince a family that heroic measures should not be used for a patient with a bleak prognosis; yet, on meeting them in the hall later, I heard the wife say, "There's the doctor who's going to save Grandpa's life." I was stunned. Everything I had said had been disregarded! The patient soon died and fortunately I didn't have to face the little girl (who will probably distrust physicians for the rest of her life). A young man at a county hospital emergency room was the most hostile patient I ever had to face. He had smashed up his car, was tied down on a stretcher with his neck in a cervical collar to prevent spinal cord damage, and was swearing and struggling, all the while smelling of beer and urine. As the most junior member of the medical team, I had the pleasure of starting an IV and drawing blood samples for this gentleman. At first he refused. Reasoning was not going to work, but after I casually pointed out that neck injuries could lead to impotence, he became quite cooperative.

A physician cannot be responsible only for the patient. A common joke heard on pediatric services is that one is "treating the parents," whose anxiety often demands action, any action, preferably a medication of some sort. (As a relatively new parent, I now understand.) Sometimes families must grieve a loss, and reactions may include physical symptoms, preoccupation with the deceased person's image, guilt about neglecting the person while alive, hostility toward health care workers, restlessness, agitation, inability to concentrate, or clinical depression.

I have just finished examining an elderly man whose life is stuttering through a massive stroke and now, after reviewing his old records, I am writing the orders. This is the easy part. Outside, in a dimly lit alcove, his family is talking in soft, bandaged voices. They are transplant candidates for hope. This time, I have to disappoint them all. On other occasions, I have been less pessimistic. But the family room next to the ICU is no place for false hope; it would only be rejected in the end after a severe reaction, a mismatched transplant.

I am rushing to an appointment, fighting the eccentric autumn winds with my coat wrapped closely about myself. This is a meeting for which I must be on time, because my patient may begin to obsess about my being late twice in a row. Suddenly, an elderly woman approaches me. She is wearing a light jacket that is inadequate for this weather. Another autumn leaf from a distant tree? She insists on stopping me, asks if I am cold. "No," I answer, "but what about you?" She's feeling just fine, because of the strawberry jam she had for breakfast. It keeps her warm, she adds. Then she takes my hands in hers, saying, "Oh, aren't you cold? Make sure they give you some strawberry jam when you get inside." After taking a closer look at my face, she says, "Are you from India? It's always nice and warm there, isn't it? No wonder you're freezing! You better get inside." And off she went, over a hillock, perhaps to give similar advice to the cold poplars. Fortunately, I was on time for my appointment. As we started talking, it struck me that I had worn the same tie at our last meeting; I made a mental note to wear a different one next time.

While strolling past a psychiatry clinic, I happened to glance inside. These people appeared perfectly healthy, no different from any other patients with minor medical problems. Returning that way, I once again looked in, this time more carefully. A young girl's hair was in disarray and she looked a little *too* casually draped over the armchair; a gentleman had just kissed an orchid with a flourish; a young man's gaze was transfixed by a blank part of the wall, as though he were having a hallucination.

A young man in a wheelchair is crying noiselessly; he seems lost among the other wheelchairs parked in the recreation room like empty shells. His mother has left, though visiting hours have just started. She is angry that he is not walking, that he is not *trying* hard enough. She has told him that he had better stop being lazy! I do not know what to say. I feel as paralyzed psychologically as he is physically; we are both helpless. When I recover, we begin to talk.

Most of my patients have external signs of disability and are very self-conscious. One quadriplegic person felt that others avoided looking at him, and another complained of people staring too much! In fact, the latter once refused to go for an X-ray, because he resented the looks some people gave him. He cooperated only when I promised his film would be taken as soon as he reached Radiology. Spinal cord injury usually results from violent accidents, and consequently these patients seem especially susceptible to psychic trauma. Part of this undoubtedly derives from their feelings about how society perceives them. During my first physical examination of a quadriplegic patient, *I* was the one who felt disabled. His involuntary movements (spasms) only seemed to worsen with my attentions, which may or may not have been desired. Fortunately, we both appreciated the comic relief when I bent over to check his blood pressure and a spasm caused my glasses to end up askew on my face!

Successful rehabilitation depends on constant vigilance and on having a safety net in medicine and the community at large. On rare occasions, a patient will find the perfect physician. One of my teachers, a blind physiatrist who also happens to be a superb pianist, once treated another musician who had sustained a head injury and developed spasticity in one hand. Her hand was beginning to take the shape of a claw, so he tested the range of motion, tone, and strength of each finger; then he began to "prescribe" certain pieces of music which could be performed in spite of her disability. Perhaps in the future, if he tries his hand at composing, he will write a piece titled "Sonata for a Spastic Hand."

In the lobby of Milwaukee County Hospital, a man in a tattered tweed coat that has been through minor surgery is smoking a cigarette, emitting erratic rings of smoke and a dry cough. Judging from his posture, his salt-and-pepper beard, and his cough, I would put his age between an old fifty and a young seventy-five. There is no more time to speculate, since I am on my way to the night shift at the ER. I keep walking, past the row of wheelchairs lined up in the hallway, slowing down only to wonder which one has been reserved for this man. When he hadn't arrived at the ER desk past midnight, I decided to go looking for him. The lobby was empty except for the odor of stale smoke. Maybe he had taken a bus and was touring the city, wearing his oversized coat like a shroud. Maybe he had gone back to whatever place he called home. In any case, I was still waiting for him, and so was his wheelchair.

At a county hospital ER, I once saw a patient with documented AIDS who was complaining of fevers. Naturally, I didn't look forward to drawing blood from this man, but I donned two pairs of gloves and did the job. Sure enough, the lab called back a little later to say "Insufficient Quantity." When I told a fellow resident about having to draw yet more blood, he said, "Just kill the fag!" I was unable to respond.

Episodes such as these occur on a regular basis in the health care setting and are often expressed through poetry. Collected here are some of the most honest and moving poems that I have encountered. I hope that these poetic articulations will help patients to cope with illness, friends and family members to understand the patient's condition, and health care professionals in their challenging work.

# The Body:
# Just Where Grace Resides

## The Music

There is music in the spheres of the body.
I mean the pull of the sea in the blood
of the man alone on his porch watching
the stars wind bands of light around his body.
I mean the roll of the planet that is the rhythm
of his breath & the wilderness of his perception
that is the immensity of light flowering like stars
in the lights of his eyes. I mean the singing
in his body that is the world of the moment of his life,
Lord!

— PHILIP SCHULTZ

## In That Year

In that year when men's bodies still looked new to me,
each one a signed, original print with one
delicious flaw I might or might not recognize,
a young man—a boy, really,
only 21—gave me the kind of kiss
you ask yourself in the middle of
*How can I move to the province*
*where* this *is the mother tongue?* —
then drew back abruptly
and spoke in that bottled voice doctors
summon when their jobs require them
to say terrible things: *Do*
*you know what a colostomy is?*
and then became himself again
and answered his own question
by drawing my hand in his
all the way down his belly
to where the warm tape held the bag
in a kind of lasting kiss
on a kind of third mouth
and told me what feeling
he did and did not have there, and finished
by peeling my clothes off like bandages, slowly,
so slowly, it seemed he was thinking
*I don't want to tear her body*
*still healing from the sight of me* —
and then turned out the light
and taught me with the miraculous
remainder of his body
just where grace resides.

— ROBIN BEHN

## Well, Pain's Wildwood Looks Refined:

a decorous everglades. And ill,
a little twister, a wasp's nest's
diligent swarm: Lord Pain. Its music, bad oboes,
calliopes fueling the Silver Flash,
the Whip, the Tilt-A-Whirl, that is the bed
with its chipped grab bars. God help us

to solariums where acoustic shadows aren't
droning keep the sunny side up, up. Give us
framed fabric edens on the waiting room walls,
the shawleries of morphine, Lourdes waters, a warm glogg
of blood in our veins. That's praying.

Try science—where hearts move
by gamma camera, old umbilical
cords make cripples more nimble and hyper-
ventilating in bags wards off
migraines. Breathing and re-breathing:

it's what we're best at. And what if
some wild octopus of the deep
comes or a big black whale or beastie
comes hellbent on gobbling us up?
Then when vespers, penicillin fail,
we'll take potluck, say please, rock me, rock
me in who cares what cold cradle.

— ALICE FULTON

## Dying Body

As the body dies, how does its beauty live?
By accumulation of indignities,
Hitting its head on ceilings, making impossible
Golf shots over shafts of trees to greens
Unseen from tees? By giving up for lost
Accumulations? Going on long journeys?
Stopping at signs? Historical Markers? Road-
side Rests? Observing observed principles
Of versifications?
               No.
               As the body
Dies, it requires strictest attention,
Nutriment, doctors, nurses,
Everyone who has given it harm,
Each person who has loved it,
All, arm-in-arm,
To keep it warm.

— THOMAS WHITBREAD

## Sound and Shadow

There seems to be a shadow. They want another
look. Can a shadow
eat you up?

*Ultra-sound*: a perfect name
for the best in stereo—the living end.
But we look more than we listen.

I lie flat, as if I've fallen.
They slather my breast with jelly
the way I've buttered a lifetime
of sandwiches. Then they move
the little mouse—up, down, around,
grazing back, forward,
the ripples just like water
opening to let the nubbin shadow through, then sealing
over, and up it bobs again, and under. Gone.

I think of the beaver who lives in our brook—
the way he surfaces
and hides and comes up somewhere you never dreamed
of looking. I want to shout

"Well, are you *real?*"
This shadow's more like a thought
than a reality. Even the thought can't hold steady as fear can,
as pain. As amputation. Un-solid, un-
dangerous. Un-serious. It will have to get my attention,
I tell it, if it wants to
kill me. No. Bravado, to be
honest. It can kill me if it wants to
any way at all.

— ROSELLEN BROWN

## In the Land of the Body (#2)

He shows me my body translated
into swirls of light on a fluorescent screen.

This is the thorax with its curving
fingers of rib, its thick
ring of fat. These
are the soft blind organs, huddled, the lungs
filled with black air.
This is a transverse section
of the spinal column: a white eye,
a dark pupil.

I'm waiting for him to read
my fortune:
values on a scale, relative
shades of gray.

Inside me everything's in color, glossy,
opaque. A lump of pain
in a hidden pocket.

His voice segmented, exact, he
talks to the picture,
takes a crayon, draws
a burst of rays
around the star he's discovered

but hasn't named.

— CHANA BLOCH

## Electrocardiogram

In the wake
of plowed snow which is always
very early, barely earthen,
it seems a city
wakes up, facing inward.
A city by virtue of its intricacy,
in which a man could
live out his whole life and still
get lost one night walking home
a little drunk. And in this line,
spired and leaping deeply,
a similar city drafts my life,
and yet has nothing
to do with my love for you, for things,
for drifts. The maps
are not always reliable;
in fact they've missed
all the palaces in which we live.

— COLE SWENSEN

## Seeing the Glory

Whatever enters the eye—shade of ash leaf,
Torn web dangling, movement of ice
Over the canyon edge—enters only
As the light of itself.
It travels through the clear jelly
Of the vitreo, turning once like the roll
Of a fish in deep water, causing a shimmer
In that thimbleful of cells waiting,
Then proceeds as a quiver on a dark purple thread
To pass from life into recognition.

The trick is to perceive glory
When its light enters the eye,
To recognize its penetration of the lens
Whether it comes like the sudden crack
Of glass shot or the needle in the center
Of the hailstone, whether it appears like the slow
Parting of fog by steady trees or the flashing
Of piranha at their prey.

How easily it could go unnoticed
Existing unseen as that line initiating
The distinction of all things.
It must be called by name
Whether it dives with triple wings of gold
Before the optic nerve or presses itself
In black fins against the retina
Or rises in its inversion like a fish
Breaking into sky.

Watching on this hillside tonight,
I want to know how to see
And bear witness.

— PATTIANN ROGERS

## How the Body in Motion Affects the Mind

Consider the mind
As it perceives the hands rising
To grasp the tree branch, each finger
Tightening on the limb and the effort
Of the arms pulling the body upward.
What pattern of interpretation synthesized
From that event
Must establish itself in the neocortex?

We know there are precise configurations
Forced on the brain by the phenomena
Of the hand clenched, by the tucking in
Of the thumb, by the sight of the foot
Flexed on the ground and pushing backward.
How do these configurations influence the study
Of duty or manipulate the definition
Of power? The mind, initiating the motion,
Must be altered itself
By the concepts contained in the accomplishment.

I could almost diagram on this paper
The structure of interactions implanted
In the neuronic fibers by the runner's
Leap across the dry gully. Who can say for certain
That structure has nothing to do
With the control of grief?
Think how the mind has no choice
But to accommodate itself to the restrained
Pressure of the fingertips tracing
The lover's spine. The subtlety
Of that motion must turn back
To modify the source of itself.

We are bound by the theorem of sockets and joints,
Totally united with contraction and release.

The idea of truth cannot be separated
From the action of the hand releasing
The stone at the precise apogee of the arm's motion
Or from the spine's flexibility easing
Through a wooden fence. The notion
Of the vast will not ignore the arm swinging
In motion from the shoulder or the fingers
Clasped together in alternation.

And when the infant, for the first time,
Turns his body over completely, think
What an enormous revelation in the brain
Must be forced, at that moment, to right itself.

— PATTIANN ROGERS

## Pollen

As when a breeze
slips off the water
and crosses a headland,
and even those limp zeroes
wavelets make, fragile as
smoke rings, erase themselves
from the viscid surface,
and sails slacken,
so the air
this afternoon slackens,
and the page blurs
under your eyes
as the massive invisible
orgy of flower
quickening flower
sifts through the atmosphere,
drifts at its peak,
rose to rose,
and from roadside locust trees
birds stagger, drunk,
daring tires,
kneeling in the grass.

Insistent as midges, grains
tease at your nostrils,
and you cry onto the page
for no human reason.
And if somewhere
a boy's arm breaks the chains
of this lassitude
long enough
to toss a stone at a squirrel,
that pine exploding into gold
tilts you toward sleep

lightly. You whisper
how wings and the shadows of
wings circle you,
surrounding the years.

— BRENDAN GALVIN

## Beneath the Skin

You linger like illness, you live
in my bones, though it's weeks
since the well-nursed fever
shivered, packed
its colors and fled.

I recall too well the operation:
you cut like scissors, clean
and to the point.

I came out slick
and dumb and I do not recover
my balance, my ease:
though my skin is smooth,
a single sheet, my fingers
do not reach, my feet are cold,
my mouth's a scar.
My eyes take precautions,
checking my steps.

And deep beneath the skin
where nothing shows
you hurt like heat.

You are the faceted stone in my belly,
the small tight clot that jerks
its way through my heart.

— MARTHA COLLINS

## Confessions of a Hypochondriac

After a lifetime insisting
that all my problems were psychological/sexual
or political/economical, according to
whichever Great Thinker I was reading,

hypochondria has forced me to pay attention to my body,
the body I've always accused of betraying me,
treated as an enemy, and hated
for not being what in others I admire.

Now it's up to me to try to get to know it at last,
release it from its adjustments to old fears
that mis-shaped it, and misused for years,
threatens breakdown at any time.

Indeed, how have I survived this long,
ignorant of what I do—
my body is as unconscious as my mind.
Of course, others I see are in worse shape,

victim to all the illnesses on the obituary page.
Don't look at others, the wise man said.
First, know thyself: You have mortal weaknesses.
It's probably too late to do anything about that,

but even so everything must be changed.
Letting the tensions in the body go
is almost impossible at this point, though—
or does that "almost" nurture a tiny hope?

No, it's pure terror that drives me,
no matter how tired, to study myself in the mirror
that tells me what I'm doing wrong or right—
warding disaster off for one more night.

— EDWARD FIELD

# The Medical Environment:
# The Hospital Smell Combs My Nostrils

## Emergency Ward

What is it and how deep? The nurse must know:
Puncture or slash or scrape or burn? There, there,
You bearers of proud flesh in single file
From the boy who holds his hand out, laying bare
The thin nakedness of bone to, O,
The stretcher case that's lain there all this while
But does not seem to care.

What in God's name was it? Fire, dog, car
That went suddenly crazy, or a power saw
That turned on its master? And did these knuckles split
Against that dumb and crooked-hanging jaw?
So nails and glass and hearts were pushed too far,
But what's a distant cause to those who sit
Nursing their new-found flaw?

Sheeted in full-length calm, the stretcher case
Stares at the ceiling while his wife stands by
Holding his one good hand. Stuck in the clock,
Time slows to ticks of pain; a child's keen cry
Ends nothing, but begins another space
Of drifting in the pale deep sea of shock
Under a long white sky.

The boy, held in by bandage, finally goes;
The stretcher case is wheeled far down the hall;
The jaw is wired so hope can still be spoken;
Yet others fill the place; the random call
Of names goes on, no end in sight. God knows
How many ways His image can be broken
And how it hurts to fall!

— LEONARD NATHAN

## At the Doctor's

Everyone could tell they had given up,
Abandoned amenities of attire, diet, soap;
She lean, face mean with fear or pain;
He obese, socks unmated, belches at the magazine
In which he looks and does not turn a page.
She would cry off and on.
They are themselves, nothing else, too far gone
To soothe our minds with any likeness
To familiar bird, beast, or fish.

An outrage:

They strung a spell over the doctor's office.
These wretches made us invisible and well,
Pick pocketed our each groomed ill.
They were so cruelly themselves, foreign and other.
Untended, their children bang and rain
Up and down the corridor like a hurricane.
They ruled the waiting room, this crude, poor pair
And they had renounced all that to us is dear.

— ROBERT WATSON

## Your Bed Is a Garden

where nothing grows. When you ask
the man for moonflowers
he turns away to dust the bladders
and rubber tubing. All night you dream
of people rolling away, while the mole
beneath your pillow
tunnels along with its feet.
When two blind eyes swivel toward you

it is daylight, and the sheets are covered
with news you cannot read.
You have come to yourself wondering
where the noise was, hoping it won't
come into your room. But there is no noise.

— PETER KLAPPERT

## The Urine Specimen

In the clinic, a sun-bleached shell of stone
on the shore of the city, you enter
the last small chamber, a little closet
chastened with pearl, cool, white, and glistening,
and over the chilly well of the toilet
you trickle your precious sum in a cup.
It's as simple as that. But the heat
of this gold your body's melted and poured out
into a form begins to enthrall you,
warming your hand with your flesh's fevers
in a terrible way. It's like holding
an organ—spleen or fatty pancreas,
a lobe from your foamy brain still steaming
with worry. You know that just outside
a nurse is waiting to cool it into a gel
and slice it onto a microscope slide
for the doctor, who in it will read your future,
wringing his hands. You lift the chalice and toast
the long life of your friend there in the mirror,
who wanly smiles, but does not drink to you.

— TED KOOSER

## Blood Pressure

The white-sleeved woman wraps a rubber
sleeve around your arm, steps back, listens,
whistles.

How it pounds in you, how it
urges through you, how it asserts
its power like a tide of electrons

flashing through your veins, shocking your fingertips,
exhausting the iron gates of your heart.
*Alive, alive, always alive,* it hisses,

crackling like the lightning snake that splits
the sky at evening, *alive,* a black rain
lashing the hollows of your body,

*alive, alive.*
You sit quietly on the cold table,
the good boy grown up into

the good man. You say
you want nothing, you'll diet, you
won't complain. Anyway, you say,

you dream of January weather,
hushed and white, the cries of light
silenced by a shield of ice.

Behind your eyes, something
like a serpent moves, an acid tongue
flicking at your cheekbones, something

voracious, whipping your whole body
hard: you're sad, you flush a
dangerous pink, you tell her

you can't understand the fierce rain
inside you, you've always hated that awful
crackling in your veins.

— SANDRA GILBERT

## How I Became Fiction

In the hospital I take care to walk
as if no destination threatened.
I drift with the cool metallic odors,
the creak of carts, the gala energy
of nurses arriving for duty
at eight a.m.

A yeast has arisen in my body.
Somewhere, a stranger's fate is being prepared,
to be typed out onto a form.

My body, see it is eager to please! and innocent
of its own yeast, its poisons and ungirlish discords!
Its product is being carried here
in a brown drugstore jar, prepared
for strangers who will not show offense.
They will charge fourteen dollars.
They will type up forms.

Death will not be simple, say the wheel-chaired
men, khaki-colored with the inertia of the wise.
They are mild beasts now, eyeing me.
*Don't stare at me, I am not fiction!*
*Not your fiction!*
My body is a girl's grown-up body, tugging
at their pinpoint eyes. My clothes are miserable
with the strain of possessing
this body so early in the day.

The men's eyes are fixed to me. But no darkness
would recover them, no alley make them male again—
*Don't look at me, I am not fiction —*
They were men once
but there is no proof of it now.
Unreal now, they brood over old skirmishes.

Like them I am drifting into fiction.
Like them I will be injected with heat and ice.
This morning, sweating, I await my fate
typed out onto a green form.
What further fiction is being imagined? What fee?

— JOYCE CAROL OATES

## In the Hospital for Tests

My mother's friend cooked for the drunk-and-disorderlies,
and so, when I was ten, I peeked at a cell,
and that's what I'd swear this room came out of—the county jail.
But here in a sweat lies a strange collection of qualities,
with me inside it, or maybe only somewhere near it,
while all the nonsense of life turns serious again—
bowel movements, chickenpox, the date of one's first menstruation,
the number of pillows one sleeps on, postnasal drip—
"It has very high arches," I hear the resident note.
He has worked his way down over its ridges and jerks,
its strings and moistures, coursings, lumps and networks,
to the crinkled and slightly ticklish soles of its feet.
"Don't worry, if there's anything going on here," the interne says,
"we'll find it. I myself have lots of ideas."

Across the room, over a jungle of plants,
blooming, drooping, withering, withered and dead,
a real face watches, freckled and flat blue eyed.
Sometimes her husband visits, a man of plaid shirts
and apologetic smiles, and sometimes three red-head
little girls in stairsteps, too scared to talk out loud.

In twenty-four hours, the hefty nurse, all smiles,
carries out my urine on her hip like a jug of cider,
a happy harvest scene. My room-mate, later,
gets on a stretcher, clutching her stomach, and it wheels
her off down the halls for a catheter in her heart.
There's one chance in five hundred she'll die in the test. She'd like
to live for two more years for the children's sake.
Her husband waits in the room. He sweats. We both sweat.

She was only fifteen when they married, he says, but she told him
she was past eighteen and he didn't find out for years.
She's wheeled back, after a feverish two hours,

with black crochet on her arm. She was conscious all the time,
and could feel whatever it was, the little black box, go
through her veins to the left of the chest from the right elbow.

The leukemia across the hall, the throat cancer a few doors down,
the leaky valve who has to sleep on eight pillows—
these sit on our beds and talk of the soggy noodles
they gave us for lunch, and the heat, and how long, how soon.
The room stinks of my urine and our greed.
To live, to live at all costs, that's what we want.
We never knew it before, but now we hunt
down the healthy nurses with our eyes. We gobble our food.
Intruders come from outside during visiting hours
and chatter about silly things, no longer our affairs.

"A little more blood, I'm on the trail." He'll go far,
my interne. My room-mate gets on the stretcher again;
she comes back almost dead, but they give her oxygen.
She whistles for breath, her face is swollen and sore
and dark. She spits up white rubber. The bronchoscope,
that's what it was this time, and more tests to come.
She wishes her husband had been here after this one.
They were going to do the other lung too, but they had to stop.

In the middle of the night her bed blazes white in the darkness.
Three red-headed daughters dangle from her lightcord.
The nurse holds a cup to her lips. It is absurd,
she is swallowing my poems. The air knots like a fist,
or a heart, the room presses in like a lung. It is empty
of every detail but her life. It is bright and deathly.

"You can go home this afternoon. You're all checked out."
My doctor is grinning over the obscene news.
My room-mate sits up and listens. "God only knows
what causes these things, but you've nothing to worry about."
In shame I pack my bags and make my call.

She reads a magazine while I wait for my husband.
She doesn't speak, she is no longer my friend.
We say goodbye to each other. I hope she does well.
In shame I walk past the staring eyes and their reproaches
all down the hall. I walk out on my high arches.

— MONA VAN DUYN

## In the Hospital

This spring it snows unexpectedly hard
and the snow seems heaviest
from inside the hospital.

Those who can't lift themselves
off their backs
ask, "Is it still snowing?"

And a nurse on the nightshift,
watching taxis spin their wheels
nine floors below, says,

"Nobody needs this, least of all me."
Postcards on the wall
show where she'd rather be.

As she makes the bed
she dreams
of her two weeks by the shore.

From rooms and hallways,
patients staring at taillights
recall waking early

to warm up the car,
living with snow simply as snow,
not as a reference to everything else.

— JOHN SKOYLES

## In the Hospital

Here everything is white and clean
as driftwood. Pain is localized
and suffering, strictly routine,
goes on behind a modest screen.

Softly the nurses glide on wheels,
crackle like windy sails, smelling of soap.
I am needled and the whole room reels.
The Fury asks me how I feel

and, grinning, turns to the brisk care
of an old man's need, he who awake
is silent, at the window stares;
sleeping, like drowning, cries for air.

And finally the fever like a spell
my years cast off. I notice now
nurse's plump buttocks, the ripe swell
of her breasts. It seems I will get well.

Next visitors with magazines;
they come whispering as in church.
The old man looks away and leans
toward light. Dying, too, is a routine.

I pack my bag and say goodbyes.
So long to nurse and this Sargasso Sea.
I nod to him and in his eyes
read, fiercely, the seabird's lonely cry.

— GEORGE GARRETT

## Visiting Hour

The hospital smell
combs my nostrils
as they go bobbing along
green and yellow corridors.

What seems a corpse
is trundled into a lift and vanishes
heavenward.

I will not feel, I will not
feel, until
I have to.

Nurses walk lightly, swiftly,
here and up and down and there,
their slender waists miraculously
carrying their burden
of so much pain, so
many deaths, their eyes
still clear after
so many farewells.

Ward 7. She lies
in a white cave of forgetfulness.
A withered hand
trembles on its stalk. Eyes move
behind eyelids too heavy
to raise. Into an arm wasted
of colour a glass fang is fixed,
not guzzling but giving.

And between her and me
distance shrinks till there is none left
but the distance of pain that neither she nor I
can cross.

She smiles a little at this
black figure in her white cave
who clumsily rises
in the round swimming waves of a bell
and dizzily goes off, leaving behind only
books that will not be read
and fruitless fruits.

— NORMAN MACCAIG

## The Hotel by the Lake

We were travelers together,
you said of those nights of false hope
when she would say, "I think this is it."
By then you were sleeping
on the cot near the door,
and the strength of her voice in the dark
was like her hand holding your wrist.
You would wake your father,
pack her toothbrush and nightgown,
and he would help her into the car.
By then she was bloated,
her tissues spongy with water,
the cancer blossoming in her body.

Each time it was the same hospital room.
"This is where I'm going to die,"
she would say, and there was nothing
to stop her from saying it
to you, to your father.
He stayed home after the first rehearsal and said,
"You go. She feels more comfortable with you."

To the end she thought
the doctors would put her to sleep
the way it was done with animals,
simply,
the way one brought the family
dog to the vet's.
Sleep in a vial on a small metal tray.
A day to plan for,
to mark on the calendar.
She told you which dress she wanted to wear.
There were mornings she woke
disappointed to find
she was still alive.

The room had no view
but at night
when the hospital was quiet
and she was asleep,
the soft closing of a door down the hall,
the dim light at her bedside,
a cough heard somewhere,
made it seem as though it were a hotel,
like the hotel in Switzerland by the lake
where the two of you had stayed one summer.
And you were simply traveling together,
your mother having turned in early
for her "beauty sleep,"
and you, up late as usual,
studying the map,
planning tomorrow's itinerary,
taking care of everything—
the suitcases packed and ready
for the porter's knock in the morning.

— CATHY SONG

## The Cure, an Anecdote

FOR CHASE TWICHELL

Once in southern Indiana where the Ohio River scallops
The border between Indiana and Kentucky, and the
     Indianans tell jokes
About the Kentuckians and the latter, as far as I know, do not
     respond in kind,
On that border, which isn't the river but runs its northern bank
Along the levee where men gather in the castor berry shrubs
To be together, once I thought I was dying. The cicadas that
     summer
Hatched in the millions and when their cycle ended with the
     same silence
As their shrieking ended at nightfall, the indignant mating
     panic shut off
As if the tranquilizer, darkness, broke the neural axis,
Another similar sound remained within me, a short in the skull
Where the nerve ran out of the brain into the right ear, and a
     numbness, too,
Like a tactile silence, edged the right side of my tongue.
To die in southern Indiana, presented with a quick sketch
Of my brain by a neurologist who drew a curve like the Ohio's
And crossed it with a bombed bridge that was the lesion, to die
Far from the Pacific my home shore while nightly my wife turned
To cry after I had fallen asleep and daily I tried to teach
The children who crossed themselves in the churches of the Valley
And had forgotten their names fixed towns and shires and
     kingdoms in Germany,
With one ear crying like a phone in a bare apartment next door
And the gift of speech held at the end of a string,
To die made me want to walk the levee where the men met
Under the water treatment plant among the mimosa fronds
And castor berry weeds, screaming and biting my tongue.
Instead of finding in the brown shallows where the levee
Dipped below the river's skin any rest, though I splashed

Cold water on my wrists and ankles, instead of understanding
The only privacy for some in southern Indiana was there
Under the bending green, I fled constantly
Those months into the whine of background noise, falling asleep
To the vaporizer, letting a fan spin beside my desk, careless
How this aged the girl my wife who lay awake plagued by sound
Or how a stranger's offered love rebuffed by fear was also
Like the body's silence that numbness parodies.
This place of average promise where the river traffic passed
And only, from its docks, pleasure craft set out, froze in my eyes
As the river did in January to an infernal lunar crust,
So that a bald tree, a pothole sunk by last winter's frost,
A round German face pocked by youth and diet, the pallor
Of the sky in summer, every average flaw beat like the delicate and
    powerful gray
Diaphragm below the male cicada's underwing, against me.
And when the tiny patch of numbness, as small as that illusion
The tongue makes cavernous in a tooth's crater, spread across my
    face,
Down my neck like a blush of terror and sank into my lungs
And the round earth fell away on every side then cupped
To fold in on this common place and this common man, hugely,
As if he mattered, the doctor put my head between my legs,
Prescribed Valium, and ordered tests begun for my dying.
And I became a citizen of the laboratory, a windowless
Country where lead lenses shielded my eyes as X-ray
Modules skimmed around my head, and technicians in accents
I understood as regional and familiar discussed
The world outside, and addressed me suddenly and solicitously
And brought picnic baskets of blood samples to my bedside
And laid me out on counters that conveyed me as they smiled
Departing greetings into cylinders of Roentgen rays,
My blood injected with a sympathetic atomic code, and my legs
    wrapped
With ace bandages (now days swarmed and grew indistinct)
And I sat with half a skull in my lap and a sharp pencil
Indicating the boney alps within where a cloud

Might be hovering, and one needle, then two, entered my spine, and
a feather
Traced the symmetries of my face and neck, and I hopped and
jogged
On one foot then the other into the doctor's waiting room,
And was asked if I was related to another with my name.
A regular to the cat scanner, full of tumors, and my doctor
Held smoked glass panels to a sunblinded window and examined
The Rorschach milk spill of my brain and remarked on the
excellence of the exposure, then turned to me,
And the fluid rose up my spine as the needle withdrew a sample of
protein,
And every nerve in my buttocks burned, and the gray route
To the t.v. monitor showed the grainy and ghosted world in my
skull
And nothing there, no tumor, only me, who, sponged coolly by the
nurse
With a seraphic face, smiled at deliverance and died with this news
into sleep.
If the Kentuckians across the river are quiet about their neighbors,
There are those who report that a citizen of southern Indiana
Is a Kentuckian who, having crossed the river, ran out of money.
I was not healed and I was. No more orchestrating the night's
Silence to an abidable wail, no more turning a third eye
To scan the wilderness inside for danger, and my wife told me
What she had suffered having saved the nights of muffled weeping
By my side to spare me and now caution me, *Never again.*
So what had happened? The doctor, satisfied not to have
To take off part of my skull and go in, said when I died
Of old age, though there is always a disease, of cancer at 83,
They would enter my head and find the damaged nerve, the
sclerosis.
It might come clear even sooner that, blinded, lamed, unable to
move bowels,
I had crossed over into a sure diagnosis.
Until then, live simply beside the Ohio River, here where
So many were perfectly happy, whose ears also rang for an answer,

Whose average bodies were speckled with invisible flaws only they
    felt.
And I thought of this, even as my tongue seemed less thick now
And the life cycle of the cicada ran down into a mumbling
Old age in my ear, that one thing we had not tried, one cure,
Was actual flight. Agreed, we chose a direction out
With a future unmarked as any floating island along
The Pacific Ocean's hazy rim, and bid farewell to friends, lovers
Of their native place still baffled that leaving like this we might feel
We were leaving nothing behind.

— MARK JARMAN

## On Seeing an X-ray of My Head

Now face to face, hard head, old nodder and shaker,
While we still have ears,
Accept my congratulations: you survived
My headlong blunders
As, night by night, my knuckles beat at your brow
More often than at doors,
Yet you were pampered, waved from the end of your stick
Like a bird in feathers,
Wrapped in towels, whistled and night-capped,
And pressed into pillows.
I see by this, the outline of our concern,
What you will lose
Before too long: the shadowy half of chin
And prodding nose,
Thatchwork of hair, loose tongue, and parting lips,
My look as blank as yours,
And yet, my madcap, catch-all rattlepot,
Nothing but haze
Shows on this picture what we had in mind,
The crannied cauliflower
Ready to boil away at a moment's notice
In a fit of vapors
And leave us holding the bag. Oh my brainpan,
When we start our separate ways
With opaque, immortal fillings clenched in our teeth
Like a bunch of keys,
And when your dome goes rolling into a ditch
And, slack in the jaws,
Stops at a hazard, some unplayable lie,
Accept at your ease
Directly what was yours at one remove:
Light through your eyes,

Air, dust, and water as themselves at last. Keep smiling.
Consider the source.
Go back to the start, old lime-pit, remembering flesh and skin,
Your bloody forebears.

— DAVID WAGONER

## X-ray

the bones gleam
out of the dark.
like the ghost of a fern
in stone here
are spine and ribs.

the skull
of my daughter is
a cup:
  something is drinking her life up.
there are islands shadowed
on her brain
  white tides are washing
    washing them out.

— CELIA GILBERT

## The AIDS Ward, U.S.C. Medical Center

Though no one speaks of hope here,
it is like the wax on the antiseptic floors:
built up layer by layer,
only to be scuffed down again
by the slippered feet of impatience.
The man in the room next to yours
has a torso covered with tattoos:
a snarling wolverine, a sinking ship,
a mermaid floating over his biceps.
As he thins, they crowd together
in a fleshy circus, a bruised riot.

Everyone's distracted.
It's clear we all hate hospitals,
detest the pretense of order,
abhor the charts and schedules,
the urgent, joyless footsteps of nurses.
But here you are, my friend,
surrounded by your fears and ours,
your mother elegant even as she fidgets,
your sister radiant and nervous as a bride,
me, destitute but smiling.
We sit around you on the patio
as if gathered at a campfire, listening
to your stories of ineptitude, incompetence,
as day drifts lazily toward darkness.

The doctor comes and goes, a little general
with his badges and neat moustache,
a technician in this Great War. And now,
I feel that I am dying too,
that this very minute I'm falling away
from the bright world,
from our words that keep breath going,

from you, whom I've loved as my brother,
my childhood lover, my soul's correspondent.
Only your terror holds me to my chair,
and your courage—the way you have
of gesturing with your fine hands,
as if retelling the story of creation,
bone by bone, feather by feather,

line by line.

— MAURYA SIMON

## Echocardiogram

Flashed on a radar screen in serpentine
sonar waves, the heart is not a Valentine,
nor a candy box, nor visceral, nor red.
Sea breakers crest and fall, wash in, recede.

> *Wash in, recede.* My heart moves linden trees
> thrums with the squall of jays, the cries of towhees.

"These are the chambers of your heart," he drawled.
"This, the aortic action. Here's the valve:
Mitral valve prolapse, echo positive.
Be comforted. It means nothing at all."

> *Nothing at all.* The heart winces and stirs,
> blazes at miracles, battens on fear.

The source of palpitations, found at last
by a black machine, strapped to the knees and chest,
that captures the echo of the heart, refines
its booming energy in sinuous lines.

> *Sinuous lines*, at least. That seaweed green
> rapture that thuds and drums and beats like rain.

"We can control your rapid beats," he droned,
without a fault or fissure. I had seen,
under the ocean waves, on a smaller frame,
green fire leap to the heart's brass kettledrums.

*Brass kettledrums.* Echocardiogram,
nymph invisible but for a song,
restore me now, but why does the heart grow numb
to the rock-faced man who died alone, despairing?

Radar angel, what of the hawk's sway,
the bulrush, marigolds, the heron's cry,
of earth's erratic lights and shadows? There
let your needle calculate disorder.

— GRACE SCHULMAN

## A Question of Memory

Every morning
the doctor with rimless glances
asks her for the date.

Forgetting backward
she disremembers this morning,
then yesterday,

reels in the years,
undoing the web of her life from the outside in.
Last winter hisses behind her brow, erased.

Caught in her mouth, a memory stirs,
the husk of an enormous moth
that crumbles at the touch.

Voracious, inconsolable, she wolfs it down,
croaks at the doctor, *I know your game!*
and scowls at the wall.

Under her door she can see the days
pass in the corridor like empty wheelchairs.
An inmate shuffles past,

dragging his walker like a portable cage.

— DONALD FINKEL

## Intensive Care

The roads to my father's heart
are newly paved.
The man who touched his heart
kissed him on the forehead
as he awakened.
Two men from the old countries,
Palestine, Lebanon,
meeting in such a carefully lit land . . .

A secret comfort to me, outside,
where I was standing and sitting
with women who read *The National Enquirer* all night,
"Infant with a Chicken's Beak,"
generously offering copies to me when through,
that at least they shared two tongues,
not one, perhaps this doubled our hope.

One woman blotted her lips
each time the phone rang
and I leapt to answer,
balanced on the tender pedestal of news.
We hovered by bedsides, gripping, five minutes only:
*You, you, you know how to come back,*
*to reach for the rail.*

Beyond those windows
trees resumed their bonier lines.
A helicopter kept lighting on a nearby roof,
blades whirling, soundless. From a distance
all things can be borne.
More than once a wild sun flooded the horizon,
igniting towers, the thousand tiny automobiles
crawling toward offices, paper clips,
crawling, with radio stations casually tuned.

We said everything good we had ever
heard of. Men who sewed their own legs
back on in the fields, who breathed twice
as deeply now. Even the couch sunk in the middle,
startling each new resident,
achieved a storied gleam. And the spaces between us
rose curling into the air like smoke
from that other room of vigilantes
who believed themselves more immortal
than we. The upended stories
and the fierce ellipsis pulsing
in our chests, so when Ricki from Texarkana
said, "The truth is, honey, they *can* die,"
she wasn't talking to us. Not daughters
sisters, not the wife with
a thin blanket folded beside her.
The ones with fists shoved in pockets
strutting past the free coffee machine
repeating Come *on*, Come *on*,
to the silver swinging doors with
electrical connections,
speaking each step and
handing it over:
*roads, not roadblocks,*
*calendars, the kiss that pulls us up*
*to many many days.*

— NAOMI SHIHAB NYE

## Two Hospital Poems

### Tools

No one speaks of the Craftsman tools
He polishes in his surgeon's shop.
Planer? Sander? Saber saw?

What sort of crowbar
Will he lean on to pry this hollow hip
Out of its socket?

I see the bone man smile
Like a Sears ad, big face and open collar,
Arms hairy among the chips
And bonedust. His fingers
Confide in the ground steel
Of the knife.

### Steel and Bone

One day I will go with hardly a limp.
Still, the steel squeaks and sighs
Against the bone. A horseshoe
Nailed to a tree and overgrown
By bark. Planted, it will
In time grow steel ankles, steel
Elbows, steel balls. A heaviness
Already troubles the joints of my tongue.
I will race my daughters again
But I carry a cold sound
In my hip pocket.

— CONRAD HILBERRY

## Convalescence

I found I could change my eyes into a fly's by staring long enough through the screen. I'd stare until I felt them start to pull and blur, then bulge out and expand, and suddenly everything would become clear again and I could see over my head, back down along my spine, right or left, the whole room without turning my head. I'd zero in on the white ceiling, moving along the jagged edges of cracks, across bumpy plaster, pocked and molehilled like the surface of the moon. And I'd be thinking. I'd be thinking about the enormous stale bubbles turning yellow in the water glass beside the bed.

— STUART DYBEK

## Edgewater Hospital

keeps a different time. Across the street, Lake Michigan folds
and unfolds light. It's dawn. It doesn't stop. The light,
the water, meet at a line we know slips into another dimension:
call it forever. They call it that in poems. But in
the linen closets of Edgewater, no matter how intense
and satiated the gift flowers set in window sun, or how
resolutely well-meaning the orderly's smile, something
unfolds, a shadow kept in a deepest crease, and it's

inevitable: we walk from the ward to the radiant world
outside with a part of us dimmed by the visit, the looking
ahead to another visit: we're darkness's octaroons.
Pain is always outside of time. I know two hands across
a face is a clock; and so my father says it's half past
cardiac, and stuck. The doctors have books that call some
futures days. It all depends. The glucose is a note
in a bottle and so it cries for rescue. Writing easy

turns of language on a beach bench is a way of making morning
afternoon. The lake's awaiting. For miles the great
lake drums its fingers—dependable
wash and beat. Like what they call in poems a heart,
they use that simile over and over again, as if the over
and over were reason enough. I think so. A heart.

— ALBERT GOLDBARTH

## Hospital View

Across an alley, opposite exactly
my window: Intensive Care Unit. At night I sit
in my dark and stare into its greenly lit
lucidity: I can almost read the x-rays hung
on the wall—two bad ghost pears, the lungs . . .
Plasma bottles glisten, beep-machines, a blur
of women and men in white frocks.
On starless nights I can read the clock.
I look because it's there. If,
out my window, I could see flax fields
parted like the haircuts of children,
if outside there were wide arenas of air,
if I could look out and up to a long sky
and study a jet's fading headlines . . . But,
Intensive Care is my view.
I never see them wheel anyone in or out.
They're just there, hooked up, in doubt,
trying to come back.—Come back, clear, still shapes;
hang on however, anonymous flesh,
even though you labor with it. I press
my own body back on my own bed, a wish
on my lips that your lives be again and again
limned by dawn.

— THOMAS LUX

## Hunter Radiation Center: Halloween

FOR KATE

It's the one thing you've asked for—your medicine now, not
hours from now, on the way home, after
this new rigmarole
of your x-rays, tests, upstairs, downstairs—
but I simply can't find a drugstore.
Back at the clinic, I can't even
find *you* again—I'm shown to
still another waiting room.
It's empty. I sit down.

People enter in couples: a man comes in with
a gray-haired woman in a purple poncho. She
crochets yellow yarn.
Then comes a handsome man, curly white hair, and a woman
older than he is. *She's* doing handwork
I've never seen; I think it's tatting.
"Madam!" calls the gentleman. He has the voice
of a Christmas caroler: bracing, sure. "What a
beautiful poncho you're wearing.
Did you make it yourself?"
"Oh, do you like the colors?"
"Blue is my *favorite* color."
I look again; no, there's no blue.
"He's legally blind," says the other man, to me,
"but he even does needlepoint, using a special machine."
"Is that tatting?" I can't help asking.
"Yes, it's tat-ting," says the man with the voice,
pronouncing all the t's.
The woman beside him looks up, and explains that
she is his sister, a widow from Oklahoma.
She says, "widder."
I've never heard that, except in the movies.

She's come for the winter
to see to her brother, and is tatting
bookmarks for Christmas presents. Tatting's
small: easy to slip into a bag.
Everything's colorful: her brother (the patient)
wears a red and white gingham shirt.

There's only one reason to be here.

The elevator door opens: the receptionist
cries out before we can see what's there.
She pushes buttons; nurses appear.
It's a four-year-old girl, brought in by her parents,
dressed as the Easter Bunny. "Betsy!"

Everyone knows her but you and me.
(You've turned up, and are waiting
for your next bout with the machine.
Absently, you finger your chest.
You look like
someone
being interrupted—
still making a point while
turning toward the persistent voice: "Yes? *What?*"
I explain about the drugstore.)
Betsy's parents tell us
that Karen, the radiation therapist,
made the bunny hood.
The rest of the costume's
a pair of pink pajamas.
"Are you going trick-or-treating tonight?"
"Try and stop her." Karen herself
sits down and
takes Betsy onto her lap. "Feel my pockets."
Candy in both of them!
The hood is beautifully made, of pink felt.

You remember the hospital pharmacy.
I find it, after a search; but they don't take
prescriptions intended for the outside.
I'm almost in tears, but you
snatch the prescription and vanish,
bursting in, somewhere, on your doctor, who
writes it up on the other pad.
This time it all works;
I get the medicine, you swallow it,
and you're finally called for your minute behind the door.

The medicine
won't help, nor will the treatment.
You don't even know how to knit.
I do,
but I'm slow—if I started a sweater for you
it wouldn't be
finished in time: and you're so tall, too—
such yards of knitting! "You're *family*," you say,
but I'm not:
*my* relatives
are short, like me—
I take you in my arms, to
comfort you, but
it is I in yours.

— ALICE MATTISON

**Patients' Views of Illness:
The Darkness within Me Is Growing**

## Diagnosis

To be touched like that
from so far, collusion
of skin and sunlight—one
ray, one cell, the collapse
of fenceworks: I feel mined,
nicked like a leaf
to a brown spot of burn
that catches the eye. Visited.

With one eye open
I probe the small swelling,
hoping to know
this intimate enemy
that bites through the bone
if left to its own
staggering devices: so this—
as if a myth had fallen
into the back garden
and stood in my light
when I took out the trash—
is it. Detached
and absolute, the word
comes over the phone
and day chills a little, ghosted,
goes briefly out of focus.
Somewhere a knife is sharpening;
my skin shivers. I can
see my own skin
as if it were
another—a dear
companion, lover, brother—
shivering, *Malignant*.

Outside
I'm swimming

through a hot storm
of light: head down
I hurry from shadow
to shadow, eyes on the ground,
where I see the fresh tar
sealing the driveway
is already cracked open with
little craters, irresistible shoots
of dandelion and crabgrass
knuckling up. Nothing can stop
their coming to a green point, this
hungry thrust towards light. Here

are seeds the songbirds will forage
as the weather hardens
before snow, green wounds
gleaming in tar, life itself
swallowing sunlight. The blacktop
glares at a clear blue sky
and in my eyes the sun
spins a dance of scalpels:
I pray for cloud, for
night's benign and cooling
graces, to be at ease again
in the friendly
land of shadows.

— EAMON GRENNAN

## Here and There

I go in and out of fantasy. I don't much like it *here,* and *there,* there is at least the possibility of magic. When you are good, you are rewarded, and the idea of bad is not the same as it is here. There, you can think evil thoughts about your mother, eat butter and meat and sour cream, and you will not get punished, not get cancer.

There, you can say the right word or the right group of words, and you will kill the wicked witch and get her house and her car and all her riches. There, you may meet a kindhearted dove or rabbit or old woman and get led through a secret door where someone will grant all your wishes.

Not like here. Here, they cart away parts of your body piece by piece and your hair and your eyelashes fall out and you collect them in a plastic bag and put them in a drawer so that you will always remember. No one will take them away and say prayers over them or make magic so that you will become whole again. Here, no one forgives you, and you cannot forgive yourself.

— HELENE DAVIS

## Cardiogram

Chances are good my number will be up
before my kindergarten son even
graduates from high school, my doctor hints,
given my scores on my latest blood test.

In the past, she let me have the Bible's full
three-score-&-ten, but now the numbers tell,
she says, a different story: I am twice
as likely as your average man to fall

victim to my heart. When you factor in
family history, forget it; my ticker
is a time bomb, as if I didn't know.

In matters of the heart I always go
strictly by the numbers, after all,
counting down to the certain end of the line.

— RANDY BLASING

## Outlook

Lying flat, under a green machine
hung from the ceiling's crossed tracks,
its big crayon-tip aimed at my guts,

I can read its big nameplate: PICKER.
Up from the box the tip comes out of,
three 1/2″ cables, flexibly tied to each other,

climb in long half-loops up a green arm
to the ceiling, before heading out
to wherever they get their power. Which

comes down to them into the box, out through
the crayon's nose-cone, through me and
the table I'm flat on, onto film

in a lightproof tray. Two of the cables
look lighter gray than the third. And slightly
kinked, where black marks show the remains

of electrical tape before the advent
of serrated plastic ties. Which now
bind in the dark third, the part

they had to replace to make the whole
machine work: so they could look into
whatever's next, whatever it is I'm in for,

here lying flat as the film that, as
it develops, will show what doesn't appear
out under plain old sky.

                  Sky. Which when I
came in, was just beginning to snow.

— PHILIP BOOTH

## Alzheimer's

I send him a gift such as a boy
might wear with delight—a bola—
pendant to place around his neck,
sporting turquoise, a blue stone
with fissures like those
of the brain or the parched earth
or a clay marble held by a boy's thumb
—for he no longer wears that black bowtie
which was always his emblem
when he circled the barbershop chair
like Samson at his millwheel
and the curls went falling everywhere
as the eager boy went sweeping, sweeping.

He will look down and toy
with this stone, hold it up
as if it were a timepiece, again
be told who sent it, mutter my name
like a stranger, not recall
the son who once wrote from a near
deathbed to say he had begged
for bread, got a stone. Even then
there had been no response—
another stone in the mouth, survival
not blessed as it might have been.

I send him stone, cracked like the sky
full of tornadoes, where lightning raged
and earth had gone withered and dust storms
darkened his eyes. He too in that season
before he learned a new trade and moved into town,
plowed up nothing but stones, earth hard as stone.

And a visit—chance to gaze into blank eyes,
hunger anew? I have not half the courage to try,
and therefore across a great desert send stone.

— DAVID RAY

## Fear of *Gray's Anatomy*

I will not look in it again.
There the heart in section is a gas mask,
its windows gone, its hoses severed.
The spinal cord is a zipper
& the lower digestive tract
has been squeezed from a tube like toothpaste.
All my life I had hoped someday to own
at least myself, only to find I am
Flood's ligaments, the areola of Mamma,
& the zonule of Zinn, Ruffini's endings
end in me, & the band of Gennari lies near
the island of Reil. Though I am a geography
greater than even I surmised, containing as I do
spaces & systems, promontories & at least
one reservoir, pits, tunnels, crescents,
demilunes & a daughter star, how can I celebrate
my incomplete fissures, my hippocampus &
inferior mental processes, my depressions
& internal extremities? I encompass also
ploughshare & gladiolus, iris & wing,
& the bird's nest of my cerebellum,
yet wherever I go I bear the crypts of Lieberkuhn,
& among the possible malfunctionaries,
floating ribs & wandering cells, Pott's fracture,
mottles, abductors, lachrymal bones & aberrant ducts.
I will ask my wife to knit a jacket for this book,
& pretend it's a brick doorstop.
I will not open *Gray's Anatomy* again.

— BRENDAN GALVIN

## The Condition

The darkness within me is growing.
I am turned out.

Thought feeds on it
even as the body is eaten.

Its goodness is without a face.
But it convinces me to look.

It can fade from now until doomsday.
It will not fade.

In the night I see it shining,
like a thing seen.

— MARVIN BELL

## The Doctor of Starlight

"Show me the place," he said.
I removed my shirt and pointed
to a tiny star above my heart.
He leaned and listened. I could feel
his breath falling lightly, flattening
the hairs on my chest. He turned
me around, and his hands gently
plied my shoulder blades and then rose
to knead the twin columns forming
my neck. "You are an athlete?"
"No," I said, "I'm a working man."
"And you make?" he said. "I make
the glare for lightbulbs." "Yes,
where would we be without them?"
"In the dark." I heard the starched
dress of the nurse behind me,
and then together they helped me
lie face up on his table, where blind
and helpless I thought of all
the men and women who had surrendered
and how little good it had done them.
The nurse took my right wrist
in both of her strong hands, and I
saw the doctor lean toward me,
a tiny chrome knife glinting in
one hand and tweezers in the other.
I could feel nothing, and then he said
proudly, "I have it!" and held up
the perfect little blue star, no
longer me and now bloodless. "And do
you know what we have under it?"
"No," I said. "Another perfect star."
I closed my eyes, but the lights
still swam before me in a sea
of golden fire. "What does it mean?"

"Mean?" he said, dabbing the place
with something cool and liquid,
and all the lights were blinking on
and off, or perhaps my eyes were
opening and closing. "Mean?" he said,
"It could mean this is who you are."

— PHILIP LEVINE

## Bypass Surgery

1

For russet
Mountains the white hospital
For lingering memories
The exacting future
For rich living the needle's eye

2

This is the bouquet
of the other life, purple stalks
and soft white umbels, orange dwarf
chrysanthemums, the fruit-freckled petals
and flared green leaves poking up
in a lovely crowd from the water of a jar
setting the *joie*
of spreading sunlight against the white
bed of my convalescence

— ALBERT COOK

## Tennis Elbow

From having fun
one way only,
doing the same thing,
the same way exactly,
grinding membranes
that once oiled
every movement,
that once made
the fluid glide
of bone on bone,
the thud absorbed,
again absorbed,
until the thin pad
cushioning the heavy
parts of me from
the heavy parts of me
crumbles, disintegrates.
From years of grooving
the stroke: bounce-hit,
bounce-hit, rehearse,
rehearse, racket back,
stroke, strike, follow
through. I know no
other way. The one trick
I know has worn thin
the cartilage,
has ground it down,
until it absorbs no more,
until I am in touch
with myself. Parts
never meant to touch
are touching. They touch
again, crush and grind,
until I am bright with ache.
And every winner I ever hit,

every exquisite triumph
has made me exquisitely tender,
put a twinge in my step,
a shine in every simple act I do.

— JIM HALL

## You Outlive All Your Diseases except One

**1**

Give me anything of value, the nurse said,
watches, rings, teeth, whatever
is removable, also your eye, leg, hair
no I said and there are no
hairpins on me either, nothing,
nothing, I am stripped
down to my self,
plucked like a chicken, punctured for oblivion,
in anonymous white worn backwards,
wheeled like secondhand goods to a stall.

Strapped under arc lights I see
a dark doctor who says he writes poetry
in Arabic. I sympathize with a kind
anaesthetist who can't find my veins. I halloo
my own doctor who like santa claus
with a black goody for me sends me
raw, split,
sailing into cushions of mercy.

**2**

Name me the parts
of cars, pistons, spark plugs, axles,
tires, doors, roof, radiator, categories
of fallibility that will be eaten
by collision, rust, attrition, age
and lie
abandoned by a used car dealer
in a hospital of wrecks.

Grass pushes through the speedy engine.
A lazy beetle
on the steering wheel

turns imperceptibly with the earth's
turning. They have lost their counterpoint of motion.
Gaping like lepers
the old cars freeze
in insufficiency: sky, weeds.

— RUTH  WHITMAN

## Malignancies in Winter

### I

The doctor's hand removes anything hard
Within the shifting folds, or any part
Already damaged or irregular—
Cells touch madness. Then they come apart.
And who began the change? Decided to choose
Hurrying, more hurrying, more ruined
Tissues; and intrusions, wider, wilder; new
Ways to swarm the softer flesh and lose

What happens next. So what? Who watches
Health, self-help, when decadence seduces?
Seasons of abandon: cigarillos,
Spike heels hurry down the freeway—such
Pretty mysteries, whenever the body refuses,
Hurrying away from all it knows.

### II

Thought erases itself against TV—
The news, with dolphin-safe Bumblebee
Tuna tonight—erased so easily
That even cinderblock distracts, the pale
Blocks I count around a pink Monet.
Thought is not I or me; not a body
Stitched, hot, and hooked to fluids, afraid.
In twilight, all the chilly flowers gray,

Those laughable touches of concern,
Delivered once with little cards, edged
With hearts and dancing red chrysanthemums,
"Get well quick!" "Get well quick!" They come
Once, tentatively; then silence returns,
Wadded in the manners of affection.

## III

The doctor gave me a stranger's blood, a scar,
And what he took out lingers in a word
That lodges, grisly metaphor
Sucking long after a body heals. If only
Fear weren't common as breathing, as I watch
The sky making color over splatters of trees.
And even after hearing, *this is how it begins,*
Still I can't predict the shade of morning

After morning, nor how it lasts: more
Light the color of surgical masks will ooze.
But now, like a color rubbing out another
After dawn, the chance of ending what
I hardly know cancels what I want—
This poem, a scar I want to make in you.

— JUDITH HALL

## The Patient

disease has expanded my horizons
and pain
spread the good word

since I've been sick
I feel close to the blighted things of nature
(I myself am a blighted thing of nature)
    burnt oaks
    gutted houses
      (for surely houses are as natural as beehives)
    broken foxes lying by the highway

    bugs crawl along the rims of my glasses
    my body pocked with spiraled holes
    like those punched in butter
    in each hole something     moving

hooked on disease (it gives
meaning to my life)    I wriggle wormlike
around the pain and God
is the large-mouthed bass circling
below me

— PETER MEINKE

## Under the Incense Tree

Come, you said to me,
read me your poem.

The sky was blue
above the mango grove,
I was distracted by its permanence,
by your hands,
smaller almost than mine
as you held a glass of water for me.

We sat on wicker chairs
drawn to a verandah wall,
half facing each other.

Only my words were between us.

Nothing trembled
in the glass or out of it.

\*    \*    \*

Before I set out to come here this
morning, you said,
turning towards me

I read the Vedic hymn to Ushas.

There were lines that run
something like this: *O Lord*
*As the hunter prepares the wild fowl*
*for feasting*

*By stripping it*
*limb from limb*

*So you ready us for age.*

\*    \*    \*

The small birds cry
in the incense tree at night

In the lightning storm
wild fowl mate in the air.

You come down the steps
into my mother's garden.
The soil is dark and old.

I pluck the incense fruit for you.

It is hard and green
it is wooden to the touch

Bitten,
it sticks to the teeth.

Until it's burnt
it has no scent

It has no scent of death.

— MEENA ALEXANDER

## The Leg

Among the iodoform in twilight sleep,
*What have I lost?* he first enquires,
Peers in the middle distance where a pain,
Ghost of a nurse, hazily moves, and day,
Her blinding presence pressing in his eyes
And now his ears. They are handling him
With rubber hands. He wants to get up.

One day beside some flowers near his nose
He will be thinking, *When will I look at it?*
And pain, still in the middle distance, will reply,
*At what?* and he will know it's gone,
O where! and begin to tremble and cry.
He will begin to cry as a child cries
Whose puppy is mangled under a screaming wheel.

Later, as if deliberately, his fingers
Begin to explore the stump. He learns a shape
That is comfortable and tucked in like a sock.
This has a sense of humor, this can despise
The finest surgical limb, the dignity of limping,
The nonsense of wheel-chairs. Now he smiles to the wall:
The amputation becomes an acquisition.

For the leg is wondering where he is (all is not lost)
And surely he has a duty to the leg:
He is its injury, the leg is his orphan,
He must cultivate the mind of the leg,
Pray for the part that is missing, pray for peace
In the image of man, pray, pray for its safety,
And after a little while it will die quietly.

The body, what is it, Father, but a sign
To love the force that grows us, to give back
What in Thy palm is senselessness and mud?

Knead, knead the substance of our understanding
Which must be beautiful in flesh to walk,
That if Thou take me angrily in hand
And hurl me to the shark, I shall not die!

— KARL SHAPIRO

# Voyage

### I

That was the year midsummer's
heatwave knocked us all
for loops: cats, squirrels

up, down, round the oak and
sycamore, mobbed the birdbath,
scratched in frenzy at the camel-

back packed earth. Birds veered
cockeyed, whomped the kitchen
window. Grass snakes frizzled

on the concrete path. That
was the year mosquitoes
failed to guzzle, as I drifted

by the parched Kishwaukee river,
caught up with my wife
and daughter for a turn around

the park.
                            Faltered as I
stepped down from the bridge.

### 2

That was the year the paramedics
strapped me in the helicopter,
pointed me to stars, in fits

and starts between the cockleburs
of galaxies, my eyes blurred up
with ghosts of mayhem, fireflies,

outcasts sifting garbage on hot
city streets. That was the year
on hold. Riddled with lifelines

in an alien bed, I thumbed the Sunday
bookpage, stared at faces of those
Auschwitz children waiting a turn

upon the Zyklon carousel—near
the last photograph of Primo Levi,
their fire-eyed witness, before

he took his life,
                                    slamming
the door on half a century's pain.


3

And this year, botched up
once again, oxygen mask in
place, heart monitor intact,

cut off from warzone static,
buzz and scuttle of the
misery out there. My wife,

my dearest friend, stroked
the blue flower round
the IV in my arm, coaxed

darkness from my eyes.
With tapestries of words
sent acrobatic sparrows

rising like last autumn's
leaves from fresh-turned soil,
wove flocks of scarlet tanagers

above gold-sovereign dandelions,
unthreaded winter hair of
willows greening into spring.

And this year, back full
circle in the summer heat,
I know for all it lacks

this world is still the only
place, and walking in a flame
of sunset I have things to do.

— LUCIEN STRYK

## Trouble

Who keeps making up
questions too hard

to answer? The doctor
who puts his finger on it

says bad eyesight might be
the beginning.

Two to six inches of ice
will take down pines

and bust the magnolia's
beautiful snarled branches.

We're afraid we're still hard
at work in our busted houses,

we haven't learned our lessons,
we still don't like each other

enough. Reason's
stake is wrong

if it thinks
it'll bury itself

in our blood-sucking
hearts, it can forget

what it's taken
for evidence. Let's take

the cure, cooling
the vapors that rise

from hot waters,
let's make provisions,

let's have the doctor
set the table with knives.

Let's every day eat the forbidden
apples even out of season,

because we can't be certain,
be certain we'll decide

to be deadly, to be thorns,
we'll take sides.

— DARA WIER

## In the Light of October

FOR V. G. M.

The long red seam across her throat
shows where her thyroid, instrument
of checks and balances within
the body's greater, delicate machine,
no longer lies. This afternoon,
the sleeve of light unraveling, she drank
a glass of radioactive iodine
to melt the last small edge
of poisoned tissue down.

Now for a day she radiates
in isolation like a minor sun,
closing the bedroom door to company;
and sits beside the the window, looking down
on ranks of cattails autumn
thinned and scoured, the Sound's
blue mantle gently thrown
around the shoulders of the cove.

Her husband, for so many hours
unable to disturb her solitude,
sleeps and wakes in the cold living room,
imagining the rose
she plucked a week ago
from one late-blooming bush:
how radiant around a central gold
the shadows held like petals, luminous.

— EMILY GROSHOLZ

## The Teacup

After the hospital, forced to study
the intricacies of snow crystals
on the window, I've come to look

closely at details, like the curve
of this blue teacup's handle,
how my finger hooks

under my thumb, lifting more
than water, steam, and rose hips,
because at any moment the phone

could ring or pain,
like a rope suddenly knotted
and cinched inside my abdomen,

could scatter porcelain chips
across the floor. Now, that's why
the cup on the saucer

is the first and last
in this house, on this earth,
the only cup that matters.

— RICHARD SOLLY

## Harm

She had only begun to get used to her body's exposures
to pain, like the insinuations behind questions: winter
asking the tree, where's your strength?—a priest asking a soul,
  where's your marrow?
              Aversions, truth, invective,
it wasn't her answers which mattered, only her lying on a bed
being administered shocks until the world grew tired
of experimenting with another bit of clay and the inward liberties.
  So it seemed.
And when the intern came into the room, asking how she was
and snouting through her chest with drainage tubes, as strong a
  desire
as she'd ever had rose up in her. She must have gestured, or he
  already knew, because,
as if in expectation, he smiled at her and stepped out of harm's way,
  backward, for just a moment.

— CAROL FROST

## I Need Help

For all the insomniacs in the world
I want to build a new kind of machine
For flying out of the body at night.
This will win peace prizes. I know it,
But I can't do it myself; I'm exhausted,
I need help from the inventors.

I admit I'm desperate, I know
That the legs in my legs are trembling
And the skeleton wants out of my body
Because the night of the rock has fallen.
I want someone to lower a huge pulley
And hoist it back over the mountain

Because I can't go it alone. It is
So dark out here that I'm staggering
Down the street like a drunk or a cripple.
I'm almost a hunchback from trying to hold up
The sky by myself. The clouds are enormous
And I need strength from the weight lifters.

How many nights can I go on like this
Without a single light from the sky: no moon,
No stars, not even one dingy street lamp?
I want to hold a rummage sale for the clouds
And send up flashlights, matchbooks, kerosene,
And old lanterns. I need bright, fiery donations.

And how many nights can I go on walking
Through the garden like a ghost listening
To flowers gasping in the dirt—small mouths
Gulping for air like tiny black asthmatics
Fighting their bodies, eating the wind?
I need the green thumbs of a gardener.

And I need help from the judges. Tonight
I want to court-martial the dark faces
That flare up under the heavy grasses—
So many blank moons, so many dead mouths
Holding their breath in the shallow ground,
Almost breathing. I have no idea why

My own face is never among them, but
I want to stop blaming myself for this.
I want to hear the hard gavel in my chest
Pounding the verdict "Not guilty as charged,"
But I can't do this alone. I need help
from the serious men in black robes

And because I can't lift the enormous weight
Of this enormous night from my shoulders
I need help from the six pallbearers of sleep
Who rise out of the slow, vacant shadows
To hoist the body into an empty coffin.
I need their help to fly out of myself.

— EDWARD HIRSCH

## Returning to the World

*Sleep is the Mother of God.*—FLANNERY O'CONNOR

When I heard that thunder, I rose up like a happy animal. The window was wide, it was a hard straight rain. I leaned towards that freshness, beyond the family photos, having just unlocked the last room to my heredity. And what did I find there—In the ruins? (The contents glistened like candy-preserved antique toys.) Greed, for material possession, which must be the top layer over some other layer of need. But there in the icing of the dreamwork, I spied the perfect arthritic bicycle, made entirely of wood, every curve, each spoke—I knew it would collapse if I touched it.

My father did give me permission to ransack the past. Might I even say he encouraged me? But it was *my* move flicked the cellular switch, self-repulsion on the structural level, collapsing the castle, setting the bones on fire, exhausted under the noiseless hum. I tightened up the reins on life itself, until my hands ached as if from a horse ride. But we know the fingers were just too eager to take, that conscience doesn't want you to cheat one bit, that life is constant in its demand for you to give, and that you cannot control The World.

From the first sign of hardening, to my birthday, nine months. Now I understand the significance of cake. The unfrosted one-layer with light. How I want it to glow in the waiting room—Healed. The unseen moves upward as the physical turns stone. *"Rise up from out your carved condition."*

Each day it grew harder to move. Positioned with pillows, I would lie in the afternoon with my eyes closed, and the sun would flood in between worlds, redwood beams grasping the whiteness. Everything so still, it was a blessing that stillness. The plum tree full of flower, a gentle feeling as sleep came gratefully wrapped in soft swaddling.

Not who to blame, not even who do I forgive, just this need to be completely held. To give oneself over, to skin the shining seed— Then to bury it. It was a long, slow rain, and it was coming from me, pulled from me, aching, until even the smallest birds bathed in it, and new life came up on its own grief. I will have slept from the Birth of Light to the Death of Darkness, and then my time is come to term, this spring. Still, I have these hours, returning to the world, while the rainwater pours, streaming over the roof of this room, and I am deep in my comforter.

— LAURA CHESTER

## The Waves

The waves break against the shore with the force
of false promises. Are they giving lectures?
Will they drone on and on like they did in the old days
before our lungs took their first breath,
before our skeletons were here to start a little history?
A streak of blue cuts through my attention,
the sky reminding me that I should look outward,
not inward at my own ruins, where everything I know
is squeezed into a few crumbling walls of limestone
dissolving beneath the pressure of years.
Are the water's little nervous breakdowns a sign
that I'm falling apart? Will my self-deceptions,
half-buried in sand, be uncovered as the tide lowers,
leaving behind shells and bits of broken glass?
Why have I trusted this entourage of shadows
that follows me after each change of address?
It's as if the shadows have voted me out of office,
and I'm no longer the candidate that best represents
their vague yearnings and subtle outrage—
they'll forever remain half-formed,
colorless imitations of the things they follow,
and like the wind wringing its hands, they'll never be visible.
As I walk here, haunting the afternoon, my voice
stuck in my throat, I worry that the Gods,
performing their subtle calculations,
will cancel me out of the equations.

— MARCIA SOUTHWICK

## Love for the Dog

Before he opened his eyes, as he lay there under the window,
he was convinced he would be able to speak this time and sort
   things out
clearly as he did when his tongue was still a hammer;
a half hour later he was once again on the chair
with all these keepers staring at him in pity and fear
and giving him milk and cocoa and white napkins.
In the middle of his exhausted brain there rose a metaphor
of an animal, a dog with a broken spine sliding around
helplessly in the center of the slippery floor
with loving owners all around encouraging him
and the dog trying desperately to please them.
He sat there proud of his metaphor, tears of mercy in his eyes,
unable in his dumbness to explain his pleasure,
unable now even to rise because of the spine.
He felt only love for the dog,
all different from the ugly muscular cat
which had leaped the day before on his bony thigh
as if it were a tree limb or an empty chair,
as if he could not run again if he had to,
as if there was not life still pouring out voluptuously
like wild water through all his troubled veins.

— GERALD STERN

## Stroke

All the long days of years lying
alone the word feels pelt of rain,
shivers of night chill, and coils
in the box you built. It whimpers.

At first light it stands, stretches
to leash-length, digs a small hole,
having learned to wait, become what
through all seasons and all faces

you can't say. Eye-brimming, recalling
the down-spiral of leaves, flushed
wingbeats and sun's joy, you lie flat
in the white yards of the clinic,

among voices low in tunnels of shade.
The word scratches, paces, softly
drags its chain over the emptied
bowl, barks. You can't call it now.

It won't hunt for you. Penned, you
wait and listen to machines digging
steadily as nails in dirt, a hole
regrettable, too deep, unfillable.

— DAVE SMITH

## Polio Epidemic 1953

I blamed the cold water in the creek.
My legs were heavy, impossible to move
With flashing steps. I struggled from bed
At dawn to cross the green and grey tile
Dragging my right leg, forcing the left ahead
Until I reached my grandmother's porch
Which faced the pasture and the red bull.
The bull bellowed when he saw me there,
His massive neck lowered, his horns bright.

I woke up in a ward of white cribs,
Glancing at other children, motionless
Behind the shadowy bars. Some merely slept.
Others had braces on their powerless legs.
I remembered my favorite story, *Sea Fairies.*
A girl my age had turned into a mermaid
And dived at once into the turquoise sea.
I told myself that I was under water
Without the silver, necessary tail.
The heaviness of water must account
For my slowness as I left my crib
Hoping to find my mother or father.
All I found in the hall was an iron machine
Enclosing a grown-up woman, making her breathe.

I didn't go to second grade that fall.
A tutor came. I learned to spell "water."
I took spoonfuls of black medicine
To build my blood, and exercised my legs
With weights hanging from my bedroom door.
I couldn't bear to hear a sound repeated,
Chalk on a board, or steps on the basement stairs,

For noise made an ugly whisper in my ears
As if I were inhabited by someone
Murmuring: "You're going to die! Why didn't you?"

— MAURA STANTON

## You Again

This time I recognize your limp.
You have aged.
The floating cartilage in your knee
makes you favor your left leg.
Your diet has left you pale
though not necessarily thinner.

If there are auras, yours is gray,
for you abhor violence,
and faint at the sight of blood.
No, it is your habit
of turning away that makes
one shoulder higher than the other; denial
creases your lips with distaste.

On the street, I hear close behind me
your uneven step.
Your long shoe crooks between mine;
I trip, curse.

Someday you'll catch up with me,
your mouth at my ear, hissing.

And you will fit yourself into me
as a corpse into its casket.

— BETH BENTLEY

## At the Y

In the pool with huge fish on the wall,
light there, and that chlorine blue,
the old women grabbed
the sides and walked all winter
up and down the water, one
with a tube up her nose and taped there,
one with a neck brace,
shrunk delicate as a child, and others—
I can't remember how many.
                              I'd watch their thin backs
breathe as they walked away.
I'd squint
from the skylights. Even a sigh
had an echo there, that sweet water
an eye with no
brain behind it to speak of.
                              They'd smile at me,
so exhausted in the locker room.
They'd smile as they
came toward me through the water
where I stood
and fiddled with my goggles, always
fogged up. Above us
the lifeguard was a high eclipse, in earphones,
his eyes rolled sideways, his body
barely holding in
another body that swayed and whirred
and wouldn't come back.
                              But I'd dive down
to a deeper nothing, pale
as a pale jelly, the kind with no flavor
just the smallest scent. I got so
I'd forget the whole business
in the same tired gesture my arms would make,
the long weight I carried

thinning out to the sound of blood
in my head, that pastoral.
                        It wasn't music,
it wasn't anything at all, only
the going and the coming and the going,
the hard breath between.
I could leave it quick. After so long, I'd
pitch backward against the side
and hang there. We wake from the dullest dreams
that startled way, and lie
down again in the dark.
                        I'd lift my blind goggles—
the boy guard folding towels now, quiet,
bored with his misery. But those women
taking it so patiently, up and down the shallow end
where danger was
exact and unending.


— MARIANNE BORUCH

## Trendelenburg Position

There I was midsummer skating on a lake,
inscribing my joy across the surface, unaware
my shadow had gone—it was somewhere
out of sight, a black naked whisper of a girl
writing her story across the blank page of ice.
Then I heard cracking, as though the presence
of this mirage startled the ice,
but it was my skin, it was the sound of my flesh
recognizing my self, back after a long absence.
In this glass-domed world of infection the body
does anything to get attention, my fever rising
to 105 then dropping to 92. I see the girl
skating, white sparks shooting from her
ankles as she curves through air,
her shadow swaying, blades not recording
the cuneiform of swirls. I see them
meeting, each suddenly finding in the other
what it lacked, something gone unrealized
till that precise moment. That's when my mind
read the frantic writing of my nerves
and woke in my hospital bed ringed by a cloud
of nurses and doctors, head low to the floor,
feet high in the air: Trendelenburg Position, used
to raise the blood pressure and increase blood flow
to the heart—all my blood in a hurry
to get to the head and rouse me
so I can know where I am
and who I was.

— M .  W Y R E B E K

# Views of Caregivers:
# Gentleness and the Scalpel

## Limits of Imagination

FOR MY MOTHER

Easy to imagine you, newly arrived
  from Canada, walking the wards,
    long, dim corridors of Bellevue,

stethoscope curled around your neck,
  a small thermometer, silver-cased,
    in your hand. *A nurse always finds*

*work*, you said—early shifts, late shifts,
  double duty in ICU, Emergency.
    You trudged up the stairs of our house,

and I helped you undress, slipping
  the soft-soled white shoes from your feet,
    hose curling around your ankles.

Easier still to imagine you at Keener,
  far from the city on Randall's Island,
    walking the grounds with Robert Chow,

the Down's Syndrome boy you loved,
  always asking what he liked best to eat.
    I see you bend to hear his answer,

his hand pressed in yours, head tilted
  to meet your eyes, your beaming face.
    In Harlem, at Manhattan Developmental,

you had the plain, practical stuff
  of healing at your hands: gauze,
    liniment, antiseptic to clean

the cuts and scrapes of retarded children
   who fell after running too fast, trying
      to chase some ball or toy.

You'd hold them as they cried
   a loud, difficult, primal cry,
      whispered to quiet them as the sting

set in, and the pain held.
   But to conjure you, thin, weak,
      leaning on my arm to walk the ramp

at Sloan Kettering takes all I've got,
   all the concentration I can
      gather without pity, or self-pity.

When I try hardest, I can remember
   your appointments at Radiology—
      you'd trade street clothes

for a thin green gown, lead vest,
   and they fired x-rays at your body,
      trying to stun what thrived

in your lung, breeding there heedless,
   dividing without caution or care,
      more reckless than I could ever know.

— ALLISON JOSEPH

## Before Going Back

Shot five times in the chest
with a .38, only a boy,
member, the Black Killers gang,
on the table in the Emergency Room,
drugged, gasping, tube rammed
through his windpipe for ventilation.
Tube through which you breathed
for him after you cracked
and spread his chest with a knife
and bone cutters, cross-clamped
the descending aorta, held
and massaged his heart,
oversewed holes in the right ventricle
and holes at the hilum
of the lung and tied his chest
with yards of silk, blood
on your face and hands
and hair, blood soaked
through socks and shoes before
it rushed down the drain.
Now you pace the Receiving Dock,
breathe the hot July air,
its trace of sulphur, hear its sirens
coming toward you.
You shake your head to shake
away your headache. You don't
ask why you remember the man
your father said was "down
on his luck," his face fallen,
two overcoats opened
to frozen wind, his arm lifted
to announce words only he hears,
or why you remember the night
you got out of your car,
walked through the small crowd

outside the liquor store
just because, you thought later,
you needed to walk by them all
without looking any of them
in the eye or speaking,
you don't think "must
be past midnight," because
it doesn't matter what
is remembered, it doesn't matter
what time it is. What matters
is the boy will live.
He'll waken, his voice
hushed. You'll be the first one
to tell him he'll never talk again,
that he'll have to walk
with a cane. He'll cry. He'll
never know how you paced
this Dock before going back
to wipe sweat from his forehead
and whisper words he didn't hear.

— LAWRENCE JOSEPH

# A Note on the Acquisition by American Medical Schools of Skeletons from India

CHICAGO (AP)—The price (of skeletons) is down considerably from a year ago. The higher price then was caused by an embargo, since lifted, on skeletons shipped out of India. "Right now we order from a Toronto supply firm," said Dr. Harry Monson, Professor of Anatomy at Illinois College of Medicine. "It's too expensive for us to clean bones and mount skeletons. In India they have an effective and cheap method."

### i   The Husband

She's of some use, even so.
When she dies, I will sell her.
It is her bones they want
for their white gardens.
I have seen them, miles
of bodies in the sun
being cleaned to bone.
In the days the buzzards
come, pick over their meals
like little men. By night,
the jackals. In a week
all is gone and the free
bones wait with the wind
in their ribs. In a time
they are gathered. Then,
I do not know. Perhaps
they are pounded and sold
for cures. Perhaps they are
worshipped. It makes no matter.
When she dies I will sell her
and she will feed me
yet again a little while.

## ii  The Dean

Dear Sirs:
Thank you for your shipment.
Our students unwrapped
their charges as carefully
as if they had been seashells,
or old books, to crumble
to dust at their fingers.
We are grateful for the thirty
you sent, and we believe
they will be happy. Each
has been given a name and
our students have already
as you read this
begun their study.

## iii  The Student

Veena, you stand small
and white before me,
your body made whole
with wires. Like a child
I name your parts aloud:
This is your femur.
This is your fibula.
And here, in your feet,
your phalanges, the
square pearls that made
your toes. And I name
the woman parts of you,
the small hips, the few
faint proportions that
tell me what you were.
But what is there here
to tell me of the way
you must have hunched
in the hot street, of

the places you must have
slept at night, and,
towards the end, in
the day. And how shall
I know the children you
might have borne, the
white cloths you wrapped
them in when they died.
There is nothing to tell me
Veena, nothing but the
name I give you, that
and the names that join
us with all men. So
I touch your arm
then I touch mine:
From shoulder to wrist
humerus, ulna, radius.
Then I touch your leg
and I touch mine:
from thigh to foot
the prayer of the bones
femur, fibula, tibia,
and I touch

### iv   The Husband

I have spent you already
oh wife. The few coins
have passed through me
and left me empty.

— LOLA HASKINS

## Older Brother

August afternoons when the sky darkened with storms
we'd climb the old silver maple
high as its limbs could hold us
and ride that wind that rocked the wren house
and turned grape leaves to their white undersides
down on the arbor. He'd lean into it
like a prow, his hair cowlicked back
seeming to stare at something beyond
our hills of sheep and junk yards, unflinching
even when rain spattered his glasses.

That's how I think he looks now,
walking on silent shoes through the wards,
delivering news to families too stunned to question
the voice that pronounces so surely
still birth or the names of cancers.
But I wonder if there is ever a father,
a mill worker with large, blackened fists
who grabs the narrow lapels of his lab coat
and pounds on my brother's chest,
demanding that he take it back.

— JULIA KASDORF

## Doctor

The patient cries, Give me back feeling.
And the doctor studies the books:
what injection is suitable for hysterics,
syndrome for insecurity, hallucination?
The patient cries, I have been disinherited.
The doctor studies the latest bulletins
of the Psychiatric Institute and advises
one warm bath given at the moment of panic.
Afterwards inject a barbiturate. At this
the patient rises up from bed and slugs
the doctor and puts him unconscious to bed;
and himself reads the book through the night
avidly without pause.

— DAVID IGNATOW

## Putting Them Down

She waited in his office all afternoon
wanting really bad to put them down.
He explained she must lose her complex
and sent her over to see a surgeon for trees.

The surgeon had a butterfly on his forehead
and began pronto to cultivate
her condition.

The butterfly would flutter when she would agree.

"I am becoming more tree-like every day," she said.
"In every way I am getting ready to put mine down."

First the earth was landscaped,
then deep drilling—
for the doctor had explained she had
long ones.

Next day she went out to see the holes
and found they'd been dug in a pig lot.

Furious, she returned to Doctor One.
"My Dear," he said, "You're getting a swine
fixation."
Meantime Doctor Two scheduled a removal
the following Saturday. And Doctor One
sent her out to the sty to eat acorns
and think.

Some weeks later she was more than prepared
and was already putting them down

when a cop in a bacon-striped cap came up
and booked her on a 344—
rooting out of season.

— WILLIAM HARROLD

## Transplant

When I've outlived three plastic hearts, or four,
Another's kidneys, corneas (*beep!*), with more
Unmentionable rubber, nylon, such—
And when (*beep!*) in a steel drawer (Do Not Touch!),
Mere brain cells in a saline wash, I thrive
With thousands, taped to quaver out, "Alive!"—
God grant that steel two wee (*beep!*) eyes of glass
To glitter wicked when the nurses pass.

— JOHN FREDERICK NIMS

## Orthopedic Surgery Ward

And what else? The rain-beaded cars in rows,
the pale, foreshortened city awash on the gray
horizon, two skeletal poplars, an unslaked sky.

On the bed next to mine, an old man dying,
adrift on a thermal of morphine. And I, less ill
by far but rancid with boredom, holding my bad

leg numb and still. The day seems like a long
choral breath—some of us are casual, some wheeze
and strain, a few are dictated to by machines.

Now the rain, and now the light comes at a slant
from the west. At night the hale lie down, too,
though a few are chosen to watch for us all,

to monitor the machines that monitor the sick
while loneliness, complacent and businesslike,
conducts its brisk, meticulous rounds.

— WILLIAM MATTHEWS

## Incurable

I recommend the oysters here! Savoring
good food helps slow me down and pace my thoughts.
   Maybe I've had a prejudice against
surgeons since my mother's operation,
but I believe you're trained not to respond
to suffering: that's why I disapprove
of Margaret's marrying you. I'm sure you think
I'm not prepared to let my daughter go,
but I'm convinced surgeons are trained to learn
how not to grieve. Look at you now—there's not
a ripple on your face to show you don't
like what I've said. You're taught to think of flesh
by feeling with a knife—as if the line
dividing cruelty from cure were drawn
so fine, only a steady hand, and not
the blundering, brave heart, could trust itself.
   I brought you here, this meal's on me, so have
the sirloin steak, the mushroom sauce is done
exactly right. After my mother's stroke
they cut the left side of her neck to clear
the blocked-up artery and get more blood
into her brain. I watched for one whole week;
her speech returned, she could remember me.
But then another blood-clot formed; her chin
drooped to her chest, she drooled, baby sound "oo"s
bubbled upon her tongue. The surgeon said
"We'll go in on the right" as if there were
some hidden life reserved inside her head
that he alone could find. He had the look
your eyes have now when he said "Operate!
We'll try to save her life." What life is it
if she can't think?—humiliation of
poor flesh, gasping its dumb dependency!
   You cut her open and her soul flew out,
leaving a limp creation, an impostor.

I watch you lift your glass, and I can see
my daughter in your hands, numbering
her ribs beneath the skin, naming the organs:
liver, colon, lungs and spleen. How could
your fingers know if *she* is lying there?
Touching like that's no cure for loneliness—
That's why I left my wife, and why I want
my daughter cherished more than hands can do.
　　When Margaret was thirteen, we visited
the lake we lived by when she was a child.
Explaining why I had abandoned home,
I said, "Mother and I have fallen out
of touch." We don't touch when our bodies touch
was what I couldn't bring myself to say.
She hugged me as the spindrift loon-calls spread
across the water with the evening mist;
then she pulled back. Softly as possible,
I put my arms around her as we walked,
and yet my love could not reach far enough
inside where love gets recognized as love.
　　Then there was nothing I could do except
protect her from my own possessiveness,
and now I must protect her happiness
from you. Maybe I'm wrong, so here's a test
to prove you too can honor suffering:
doctors have professional ways of easing
people out of pain. Release my mother
from the dungeon of her bones; give me a pill
to rescue her. Margaret need never know;
I won't breathe one small sound of what we've said,
but I'll know that you're capable of love.
You'll have a father's blessing if you do.

— ROBERT PACK

## Vital Signs

All night, our doors
are cleft by blades of
light, and we wake
three, four times to
this nurse or that
shining her flashlight
in our faces: blood
pressure, temperature,
pulse. All night, their
shadows slip past
our doors and stop at
one room or another
down the hall where any
one of us, calling,
adores the stranger who
answers more than wife or
lover: the silhouette
immediate, anonymous, that
looms in the door. Squinting,
we swell with beatitude:

                blessèd

be the soothers of pain at
two, three, four a.m.
and the balms they
minister— pints of rubbing
alcohol, Darvon rattling in
one-ounce cups, a bead of
morphine at needle-tip.

— JIM ELLEDGE

## Monet Refuses the Operation

Doctor, you say there are no haloes
around the streetlights in Paris
and what I see is an aberration
caused by old age, an affliction.
I tell you it has taken me all my life
to arrive at the vision of gas lamps as angels,
to soften and blur and finally banish
the edges you regret I don't see,
to learn that the line I called the horizon
does not exist and sky and water,
so long apart, are the same state of being.
Fifty-four years before I could see
Rouen cathedral is built
of parallel shafts of sun,
and now you want to restore
my youthful errors: fixed
notions of top and bottom,
the illusion of three-dimensional space,
wisteria separate
from the bridge it covers.
What can I say to convince you
the Houses of Parliament dissolve
night after night to become
the fluid dream of the Thames?
I will not return to a universe
of objects that don't know each other,
as if islands were not the lost children
of one great continent. The world
is flux, and light becomes what it touches,
becomes water, lilies on water,
above and below water,
becomes lilac and mauve and yellow
and white and cerulean lamps,
small fists passing sunlight
so quickly to one another

that it would take long, streaming hair
inside my brush to catch it.
To paint the speed of light!
Our weighted shapes, these verticals,
burn to mix with air
and change our bones, skin, clothes
to gases. Doctor,
if only you could see
how heaven pulls earth into its arms
and how infinitely the heart expands
to claim this world, blue vapor without end.

— LISEL MUELLER

## Nuns at Birth

This wing is quick with nuns. They flock and flutter,
Their habits whisper, sweeping the corridor.
The mildest human sound can make them scatter
With a sound like seed spilled on the immaculate floor.

They know about waste. They come with disinfectant,
Troubling the peonies bursting on my sill;
Their quick white hands can purge the most reluctant
Stain, and the sprouting germ, and the alien smell.

Old men have said—and my anxious, Baptist mother—
That purity is the fallow ground of love.
It is here in the sterile sheets and the smell of ether,
And their bead-bright eyes. But what are they thinking of?

Or that Superior Mother about her labours:
What discipline could inform so bland a nod
When I shrieked and he shrieked and the bursting fibers
Gave him up to her quick white hands in blood?

Or the dove-grey novice now in her sterile plumage,
Who will go about birth, and about it: his hot greed
And my thickly weeping breast—what sort of *homage*
Brings her white hand fluttering to that bead,

Because it is that, my love! Her breath has quickened
At the noise of his pleasure in the immaculate air
As if some glory sanctifies the fecund!
Well. Twenty centuries' lies are brought to bear

In her innocent misconception; the germ sprouting
In the cell, the chalk on the alien door, the hot
Salvation of witches, the profits and the prating—
We have not bought those lies. But we must have

Some lies. We are consumers, you and I
and now this third, gums leech-fast at my breast,
Whom we shall wean to an epicure, and say:
Self-sacrifice is ingratitude, is waste;

And say: husk the kernel; feed at the fountains;
Seek sun in winter at the belly of the earth;
Go to the east for splendour, the north for mountains;
And always go to the nuns in time of birth.

— JANET BURROWAY

## Vapor Salve

When a fever made time crooked
and light all crossed against itself,
and breath was shrunk to raw choking
on salty fat, Mama got down
the silver tin from the mantel.
The salve looked like greasy ice, smelled
of blizzards from the little can.
She rubbed the resin on my heart
and I felt at once the needle sting
and thrill of weather soaking through
tight heat. Crusts and dumplings broke.
But what I noticed most was blue
spirits rising from my skin, scents
of pine and gum, a clear ghost swept
out through the air and opening
corridors and bright ledges,
letting in new air and stretching
time like smoke to where it becomes sky.

— ROBERT MORGAN

## The Doctor Rebuilds a Hand

FOR BRAD CRENSHAW

His hand was a puppet, more wood than flesh.
He had brought the forest back with him: bark, pitch,
the dull leaves and thick hardwood that gave way
to bone and severed nerves throughout his fingers.
There was no pain. He suffered instead the terror
of a man lost in the woods, the dull ache of companions
as they give up the search, wait, and return home.
What creeps in the timber and low brush
crept between his fingers, following the blood spoor.
As I removed splinters from the torn skin
I discovered the landscape of bodies,
the forest's skin and flesh. I felt
the dark pressure of my own blood stiffen within me
and against the red pulp I worked into a hand
using my own as the model. If I could abandon the vanity
of healing, I would enter the forest of wounds myself,
and be delivered, unafraid, from whatever I touched.

— GARY YOUNG

## The Persistence of Memory, the Failure of Poetry

In 1979, a New York high school
music student, Renee Katz, was pushed
in the path of a subway train.

The severed hand flutters
    on the subway track,
like a moth. No—

it is what it is,
    *a severed hand.*
It knows what it is.

And all the king's doctors
    and all the king's surgeons
put hand and stump together

again. Fingers move,
    somewhat. Blood circulates,
somewhat. "A miracle!" reporters

report. But it will only
    scratch and claw, a mouse
behind the bedroom wall. We forget.

At four a.m. the hand
    remembers: intricate musical
fingerings, the metallic

feel of the silver flute.

— ROBERT PHILLIPS

## Domestic Life: Nurse and Poet

FOR MARY

We talk tonight as if tomorrow will be the same,
as if we'll rise at six to get the children off,
then work the day—I with words and students,
you with the sick, the dying, and their desperate families—
until we come home at five to unleash the dog
and feed the children. We expect we'll read to them,
shush them resisting off to bed, sit here on the couch
to talk once more. We are thirty-three, but the world
mistakes you always for six or seven less.
Tonight you smile—nobody died today.
Beneath your eyes only inches away,
I catch for the first time tiny marks,
hairbreadth engravings of a stylus on copper.
On another they would be lines,
but on you, tonight, while we consider tomorrow
and who can hurry home to meet the plumber,
they are the tightening muscles in my gut,
the faults in the deepest beds of rock.

— STEPHEN COREY

## "Bed Tablets"

I had been noticing that my sleeping quarters were beginning to look a little shabby lately, so that it was quite a relief when I went to the medicine cabinet and the label on a little bottle of white pills caught my eye. It was marked "Bed Tablets." So, to begin to neaten up the room, I went back to the bedroom and sprinkled Bed Tablets all over my cot and went to sleep on the floor, to allow the room time to recover. And sure enough, the next morning, I noticed a great improvement in the room—in any case, my bed was certainly beginning to look a whole lot better to me! So, lately I've been wondering whether—no questions asked of course—my doctor might be willing to write me out a prescription for "Wall Cream."

— MICHAEL BENEDIKT

## Peau d'Orange

We barter the difference
between black and gray.
"Surgery, radiation or
death," you say and leave
the decision to me,

while I insist you are the gods
I believed in as a child.
I prayed you to pull magic
out of your black leather bags
to wave away the rattling
in my bones.

I accept your calling
my breast an orange peel,
let you lay hands on this fruit
my mother said no man
must touch. In this disease
there is no sin.

If you lift the chill
that unravels my spine,
I will send you stars
from the Milky Way,
send them spinning down,
dancing a thousand-fold. Please
let me grow old.

— MARCIA LYNCH

# For a Teacher's Wife, Dying of Cancer

Four-fifteen: a weak snow starts to blot
The city's likeness. I know you are dying.
By tonight chained tires will be churning it,
Headlights plunging into it. No planes will be flying
South from Boston. They will squat in rows
Staring at the snow that grounds them. The mewing
Sea-birds blown inland incuriously rise
Through it all, scorching the flurry with furious eyes.

Your dying glows in my brain: dry light spreading
Through the nerves, converting the cells like cancer
The crab, that pinched your lung once it set in.
I hear the lie scratch like an old record when you answer
You are feeling fine. On the phone your voice
Could almost be a ghost's, half-heard in the tense air.
I dream an ice-storm, poles crashing,
Hot wires sparkling where they loop and cross.

Down South it must seem warm enough for your walk
Today. When your husband asked us over for a drink
You would meet us in your funny walking shoes and sulk.
We talked the modern world to arm's length—
Fireside Agrarians; not even cancer
Could usurp the house's form. You shrank
From our courtesy to closet with the stranger
Whose passion banked your eyes of their gutted fire.

A man can't live in a house with death, your husband
Told me. We shooed the screech-owl off the roof.
But in this lying and cobalt time, when the doctor has been
Made a god, I had hoped to offer you truth.
The storm beats down the birds with an iron grace
And my warm words freeze and shudder in my mouth.
The snow swallows my reflection in the window glass—
I can't remember your face.

— RICHARD TILLINGHAST

## The Revenant

Last night, rummaging for scissors
in a back drawer, his fingers touched
something alive, not alive,
a pouch concealed under papers,
an envelope with no address.
In it, a lock of graying hair,
lopped from her head before the Cytoxin, cure-all,
not able to save her,
had struck her bald.
His hand now cradled one part
that had sprouted from her body,
many times assenting to
the touch of his fingers.
Her hair! The only frailty
she'd admit to! Her doctor,
never lowering his eyes,
told her she had a year to go,
adding of course he could "make her
more comfortable" with chemotherapy.
Her hands flew to her head, frightened birds
to save her hair. They fell at once
fluttering to her lap. She had to laugh
at herself, the hands. But not at the hair.
"I'm sorry," she said, aghast at her own reasons.

— PETER DAVISON

## Doctors

They work with herbs
and penicillin.
They work with gentleness
and the scalpel.
They dig out the cancer,
close an incision
and say a prayer
to the poverty of the skin.
They are not Gods
though they would like to be;
they are only a human
trying to fix up a human.
Many humans die.
They die like the tender,
palpitating berries
in November.
But all along the doctors remember:
First do no harm.
They would kiss it if it would heal.
It would not heal.

If the doctors cure
then the sun sees it.
If the doctors kill
then the earth hides it.
The doctors should fear arrogance
more than cardiac arrest.
If they are too proud,
and some are,
then they leave home on horseback
but God returns them on foot.

— ANNE SEXTON

## On the Subject of Doctors

I like to see doctors cough.
What kind of human being
would grab all your money
just when you're down?
I'm not saying they enjoy this:
"Sorry, Mr. Rodriguez, that's it,
no hope! You might as well
hand over your wallet." Hell no,
they'd rather be playing golf
and swapping jokes about our feet.

Some of them smoke marijuana
and are alcoholics, and their moral
turpitude is famous: who gets to see
most sex organs in the world? Not
poets. With the hours they keep
they need the drugs more than anyone.
Germ city, there's no hope
looking down those fire-engine throats.
They're bound to get sick themselves
sometime; and I happen to be there
myself in a high fever
taking my plastic medicine seriously
with the doctors, who are dying.

— JAMES TATE

## One Too Many Mornings

FOR STEVE

After working the midtown ambulance night slot,
my brother drinks in a tavern, his back to thin bars
of lacquered sunlight, venetian blinds. In jeans
and a flannel cowboy shirt, & trying to down-shift
enough to head home. He sips a bourbon.
It carries him a little ways off,
not far enough. How can I get out, he thinks.
On the raised television, an ugly, yellow, manic cartoon bird
keeps escaping its cage,
only to be recaptured. No sound. But his partner, Franco,
jokes about this brunette emergency room nurse.
How she doesn't wear panties, how she asks
*Does that mean you like me?* when he stares too long.
My brother has heard it all before,
so the reply is an echo. One bad joke
then another. It's like asking *why*
when you know the one right answer is to repeat
the question. Why, last night, at the Hyatt

glitter palace, he had to pull a limp twelve-year-old
from the heated, chlorine-stinking swimming pool.
He fingered the carotid for a pulse. It was there,
it wasn't. Some blood flecked an earlobe.
Kitchen noise, banged pots. Shouts from a distance.
Then a small crowd, uneasy murmurs.
When he locked fists & struck the boy's chest,
trying to make the heart flutter, switch on,
the rib cage cracked. A grunt came from the mouth,
a laugh, then silence. A laugh, he said. That's
what he remembers. Nobody
shut off the pool lights. The warm blue-green
planets under water became more
and more still, simplified & quiet.

Like a man in a bar who just doesn't want to talk,
because there are many wrong answers,
ways to soften failure. And no one wrong or close
enough, no one as far away as he is.

— DAVID RIVARD

## Biopsy

Men tracing with their mouths
scars across my breasts, each

only a little planet with its
single star, a place for sleep

& space their hands move over
well beyond the precedence of

ridge, that tumult of Van Harn's
inscrutable work, the salted

almonds of his knuckles instantly
perceived among the shining.

Vertigo of measurement in a lab
as content separated from space

the way a local swan is reflected
in a river. Then altered

variation returned (men always
working) in the rosemary

anesthetic sweat. Through that
season, God's dear cold breath

across the populated water.

— EVE SHELNUTT

## Care Giver

Father tugs on his leash all day, tires her.
Although he doesn't speak well anymore,
he can still say "no" like a tough old cur-
mudgeon: "You're cra-a-a-azy!" coming from a store
of expletives. Thus said, he refuses his
insulin shots till *he* is ready. Drinks
pills when *he* wants to. Will not shave. Piss
scrawls down his pant legs and wets his socks. He stinks,
but if she insists he change, he'll not. "How
you take this," I console mom, care giver.
"He's an old dog, isn't he?" She shrugs, her
lips tight. But now I see, she no longer kow-
tows to him, growls over a new-found bone:
"You listen—or else I'll toss you in a nursing home."

— JULIET S. KONO

**By Health Care Workers:**
**Dissecting the Good Lines from the Bad**

## The Barking Dog

There is a woman
in a hospital
barking like a dog.
The nurses know
it's the sound
of her lungs going
and her heart.
Visitors think
it's a dog outside
chained to a tree,
the rope too short,
no water,
no one passing by.
All day and all night
visitors worry.
*Why doesn't someone*
*bring in that dog?*
People give the dog
names, patients ask
if anyone can see the dog
through the window.
When the barking stops
everyone is relieved.
Elaborate endings are told—
how the dog
was taken to a farm
and set free.
How the dog
drinks from a stream
whenever it wants.
The nurses
say nothing.

But every nurse knows
the story
of the barking dog.

— CORTNEY DAVIS

## Visiting the Lightning Struck

I imagine Moses, his tablets burned by God,
but this is nature's wrath: a man
whose skin is charred with ragged ports
where bolts raged, piercing heart and lung.

Unlike holy, dead-aimed strokes,
this summer lightning flash
fused his corneas like opaque glass
and burst his eardrums, as if they were balloons.

Did fear come with, before, or after?
And did he see, or simply feel, bones smoke,
eyelids fuse? When heart stopped,
did he gasp and wait until the tick resumed,

or did the lungs freeze first, then
the other organs fail? How will he think
of picnics after this, how love
August's hazy light where bees drone air

thick as saturated gauze, until clouds
swell, random ions shift and currents
surge to kiss the ground. They say
he throws off blankets, wants all curtains

drawn. I smell his burns across the hall.
Fearing, yet praising, earth's capricious will,
I wish him trust for fitful skies once more.
I say his name. I knock upon his door.

— CORTNEY DAVIS

## Alabama

In the ward
behind a curtain
with a sleeping cap
akimbo on her wig,
Alabama whispers
like a locomotive,
*Let me go.*

In some brown place
above her bed,
my stern professor stands
and frowns
at my attempts
to stoke the boiler
in her chest.

Wrinkled and abused,
this Alabama lies
in some deep structure
of my mind where still I kneel
beside her freckled arms
pumping morphine, merc
and oxygen.

The distant locomotive chugs.
I slap her, *Dammit,*
*Live!*

— JACK COULEHAN

## Emergency Room

Bum rap tramp dumped at the door.
An ashen somebody's something
With a somewhere cousin or brother.
A bag of smelly sticks ready for the pyre,
Last round, set 'em up Joe, dextrose-saline,
Vintage 77, dash of bicarb, Aramine bitters,
A 400 watt bang-bash rum fit
With a dissociative sociopathic EKG.
His—our failure? What the hell,
Shock him one more time
This one's for auld lang syne.

— HOWARD B. PERER

## Baby Random

tries a nosedive, kamikaze,
when the intern flings open the isolette.

The kid almost hits the floor. I can see the headline:
DOC DUMPS AIDS TOT. Nice save, nurse.

Why thanks. Young physician: "We have to change
his tube." His voice trembles, six weeks

out of school. I tell him: "Keep it to a handshake,
you'll be OK." Our team resuscitated

this Baby Random, birth weight
one pound, eyelids still fused. Mother's

a junkie with HIV. Never named him.
Where I work we bring back terminal preemies.

*No Fetus Can Beat Us.* That's our motto. I have
a friend who was thrown into prison. Where do birds

go when they die? Neruda wanted to know. Crows
eat them. Bird heaven? Imagine the racket.

When Random cries, petit fish on shore, nothing
squeaks past the tube down his pipe. His ventilator's

a high-tech bellows that kicks in & out. Not
up to the nurses. Quiet: a pigeon's outside,

color of graham crackers, throat oil on a wet street,
wings spattered white, perched out of the rain.

I have friends who were thrown in prison, Latin
American. Tortured. Exiled. Some people have

Courage. Some people have heart. *Corazón.*
After a shift like tonight, I have the usual

bad dreams. Some days I avoid my reflection in store
windows. I just don't want anyone to look at me.

— BELLE WARING

## Night Watch

In a far corner of the ICU waiting room
the ancient rusted-grey radiator
has been wailing all night: a pounding
squall, followed by high-pitched shrieks.

The three of us, near strangers,
lined up along the wall
in scooped-out fiberglass chairs, pitch
our voices just loud enough
to be heard above it. Sipping coffee,
we speak of heart attacks and cancer,
calling messages to one another
as if across a frozen lake. Then each of us,
in courteous sequence, glances up
at the clock that rules the opposite wall.
One by one we cross the room,
walk toward our own reflection in the dark
curtainless window—first the elderly
man in the green plaid coat,
next the mother clutching her fistful
of tissue, then me.

Below the window, a line of thin figures
slips elusively between trees, turns
into headlights sweeping
the parking lot fence. The long,
long shadow of the night watchman
grows shorter, shorter as he approaches
a streetlamp, his breath
ghosting the air. Down the hall,
you swallow oxygen through a tube.
In an hour or so, day will start throbbing up,
mirrored on our faces, glinting off
windshields.

I turn in time to see the young man
in a blue coat, oil-stained,
nod as he marches across the room. He kneels
in the corner before the ailing radiator,
and then, with a wrench, reaches in.

— DAVID LANIER

## A Pause

What did the test show, his daughter asked.
There was this momentary pause, an amount
of time to delay still acceptable, maybe
one and a half seconds, or so. That's the gap

in which I've no conscious thought. I don't
plan what I'll say, but it must be a time
these neurons need to dwell over the answer
internally. I see how the mouth is framed,

just the way the lips are left parted, how
the head is tilted slightly down and pupils
widen. I see her hands cupped around
the chair's arms, fingers pulled in tight,

feet pulled deep underneath.
Her pocketbook, large and full left
on an exam table, the x-ray envelope
nearby. She could see the name

on the cover, could see writing
if she wished, that said CT of brain.
But she doesn't look that way. She looks
hard at me while I pause ever so slightly.

— MARC STRAUS

## Questions and Answers

"Why complain," the old Jew
always says. The Irish man
says nothing. The Black man
seeded with pain from the prostate

tumor withholds, says less
than is so—until that day,
maybe after you've held his arm,
touched him gently, that he'll look

at your white face, and ask
a question. The question
might be so simple, so clear
that you're unprepared to answer.

— MARC STRAUS

## Vita Brevis

Did you know butterflies were tenacious.
They do not die easily; they suffer
Captivity more than most creatures
& entertain scarcely a flutter from
Enclosures. Perhaps it is
Their drab full past which prepared them
Excellently—the crude beginning;
One death, an entombment:
Change of a spectacular sort—
And resurrection.
So that—reborn—they treasure
& defend this fragile existence as it is . . .
And are loathe to leave again.

— DORIS VIDAVER

## Magic

The end of another day
                a very confusing day
The day after a holiday
                kept thinking it was Monday
                on this feverish Friday.
Case after case mixed in the blender.
A montage
        of heads
        bodies
        limbs.
I find it difficult to concentrate
           on one particular case
           on one definite face.
But it was a good day.
The sick ones that I saw
the day before were well.
Today the magic worked
Tomorrow
well that's another story.
I'll sip my tea.
Then I'll wait
and see
and hope
expectantly
for the magic
to begin again.

— LOUIS ALPER

## Surgeon

The instruments have fine balance.
The slap of a cold hemostat
against a rubber glove speaks.
Take it. Clamp it.
Grasp and swirl black silk
around the steel tip
to tie the severed vessel.
Curve the Metzenbaums and tease
the tissue planes apart, hover above
an alert Carotid, gently retract
that fat blue Jugular to trace
the Vagus, cleanly on course.
Quicken your fingers in silver and red,
completing the hidden architecture.

Now, poised between the act and words,
emerge, secure with lowered mask,
leaving form to face the family.
Questions pelt from the babble of faces:
"Is it over?" "Will he live?"
"Did you take many stitches?"
"How long is the scar?"

Grope for steady answers.

— HAROLD QUINN

## Amnesia

Three days black: the day of the fall
and one on either side. The crack
in your skull is leaching lime

to put back into place all
the mind that leaped out like a pack
of frenzied dogs. For you the time

since that misstep on the ledge
is a mirror that follows you back and back,
but leaves you at the edge.

— JOHN STONE

## Getting to Sleep in New Jersey

Not twenty miles from where I work,
William Williams wrote after dark,

after the last baby was caught,
knowing that what he really ought

to do was sleep. Rutherford slept,
while all night William Williams kept

scratching at his prescription pad,
dissecting the good lines from the bad.

He tested the general question whether
feet or butt or head-first ever

determines as well the length of labor
of a poem. His work is over:

bones and guts and red wheelbarrows;
the loneliness and all the errors

a heart can make the other end
of a stethoscope. Outside, the wind

corners the house with a long crow.
Silently, his contagious snow

covers the banks of the Passaic River,
where he walked once, full of fever,

tracking his solitary way
back to his office and the white day,

a peculiar kind of bright-eyed bird,
hungry for morning and the perfect word.

— J O H N  S T O N E

## Chromatic

I take off my white coat—
Emerge from the world of white and black
And shades of gray
To touch the grass.
To walk the street like others.
No cloak of reason
Constrains my every step.
I laugh!
The bounce returns to my walk.

I try to forget:
The babies crying in the night.
The motorcycle riders
Who never return home,
The rape,
The beaten wife.

Off with my white coat.
I, too, wear jeans and sneaks,
And reds and blues;
Walking among the leaves
I see the sun.

— STACY J. KEEN

## Driving Home from the Clinic

On the narrow back road to Monroe, after rain,
the air was a bittersweet tea
of mayweed mixed with the creek, wild onion, and pine,
the freshly turned earth like a root split open,
then held to the nose.

I drove home slowly, with the windows rolled down,
and I listened to the hush of the tires
on the damp asphalt,
felt the patches of cool air washing my arm,

saw a farmhouse lighted by a single yellow bulb
and drifting far out in a field
as dark as the bottom of a lake, while the clouds
to the southeast blossomed with lightning.
                                                God,
it was all of this, even
the smell of a polecat killed on the road
mingled with the wild sweet olive, this
and the news,
that compelled me to know, for the first time,

that I want to grow old,
to entertain grandchildren, telling true stories
that surprise them at the end,
stories of things long past, yet to happen.
To be able to say:

*The night it all started, there was jasmine*
*floating on the air.*
*There was mica in the wet road, glistening. Cicadas*
*had remembered how to sing.*

— JUDSON MITCHAM

## Vermont Moment

Quiet, broken by nothing but winded trees
and an occasional, but a very
occasional car opposed by the breeze

to silence; and the usual hopeful birds,
which really belong to the silence.
I touch the back of Thoreau's *The Maine Woods*

on the antique bookshelf, blessing our new
discovery, this house. Hung from hand-hewn beams
above stone and plank-oak floors, with a few

things from Thoreau's time he might even like—
our place for the summer. I turn from the book
because something little has touched me, like

a child's hand; I can almost hear laughter.
The infant rocking chair of a child long dead
moves on its own. Moved to sit and watch, after

eight years of deliberate childless dread,
I rock, and watch the tiny rocker rock,
our talk, about you conceiving, in my head.

— MELVIN KONNER

## Listening In

The thin heartbeat chuffs at us through wires.
You start to cry and laugh at the same time.
Even charged through hardware, it inspires,

announcing its *I am* to expunge doubt.
Muffled in Medsonics scratches, belly
glugs, and your own uterine whoosh, it's out

reluctantly, as it will be born
later, by the bone. Reluctance reigns here,
a kept counsel, even a sort of scorn

of emergence, of society.
Are those fetuses in pictures sucking
thumbs, or thumbing noses? As the we

that is us is stretched to make room for it,
it takes no notice of our sacrifice.
It gives this tiny thumping, yet we love it;

it can't help itself if it's so small.
It's corn, we know, but are not above it,
and have long since sunk into its thrall.

— MELVIN KONNER

## Epilogue

Now, after many years of caring for the sick,
I sometimes think on how it all began,
and how I undertook the ancient craft
that had its origin in chant and rite,
in tribal shamans, augurs, oracles and priests,
apothecaries, alchemists and quacks.
This is the lineage I lived each day
in varied acts some men are pleased to call
a science.

God has been very good to me
in granting some small feeling for my art,
for untried knowledge is a fickle friend.
A current fact is often next year's myth
since what we "know" is sometimes less than true,
while what we need to know compounds itself,
accumulates at rates of usury
such as to beggar us, our mouths agape.

The years bring obsolescence to us all.
An old man values as patina
what is rust and crumble at his age;
the pride of old achievement lasts too long,
and art, unaided, makes for charlatans.

To blend a timeless craft with knowledge is
supreme; then wisdom slowly grows with time,
like coral, quietly beneath the waves,
builds islands in a far-horizoned sea.

— SAMUEL STEARNS

## The Son: Returning Home

FOR SUSHIL KUMAR ERIC MUKAND

Moist air crystallizes into morning, shimmers
in the sunrise, cutting my face as I leave the house,
as I leave you.
                    You are the medical texts,
the pipes scattered about in empty ashtrays, the sunlight's
dull reflection from the antique brass lamp.
You are gone, resolved
in an electric moment to urned ash, leaving behind
a stray sitar note which resonates
in me with its saffron music.

The respirator's measured, regular breaths
replaced your own cigarette-scarred wheezing.
You tried to quit, but keep on borrowing
cigarettes from patients, as if a smile
was enough payment.

The peaceful hiss and sigh
of your plastic lungs
was incessantly regular.

I tried imagining the incinerator,
but during the funeral
my memory could only filter
the burned fragrance of cumin and cardamom.

Why do we need oxygen
to live and to die,
for metabolism and for combustion?

Was your life
a poorly controlled chemical reaction,
and its by-product your death?

Once, under the heat
of the Indian sun, you lifted me up
to the branches
of a mango tree, caught me when I jumped down.
Now I am left with the fruit of long days,
nights away delivering babies: your heart on
crutches, arteries rusted away.
And you knew, you knew.

90 percent occlusion
of the anterior descending artery,
80 percent of the circumflex.

Hints of self-diagnosis in journal articles
you underlined: *coronary bypass, cardiac
catheters, myocardial infarctions.* Reading
your medical records, I also knew.

We can only walk so far away from home,
from our fathers, who have left us
their lives in each dying cell, each spiral
DNA staircase that ascends
or descends to the next day.

The house holds me
like a kite, reeling me in, taut
against the gusts blowing on this bamboo frame.

You will be waiting:
wire-rimmed glasses, trim moustache, smiling
with my mother, a photograph on the night-stand
before I turn off the brass lamp.

So I turn
homeward, promising to write
a *ghazal* for which you
have left behind a melody.

Someday, I will hear the *tabla,* whose rhythm
no EKG can capture and no cardiologist
can interpret. The music will
take me back to the lotus pond
at our old home in the village of Sultanpur:
then, I will drift away on the fallen petals.

— JON MUKAND

**Family and Friends:
Afraid to Name This Dying**

## The Hospitals

It's the season they take the fathers to hospitals.
Wheeled off half-mown lawns, found in cellar-rank
Family rooms, the fathers are sped to Emergency

Where nobody hopes the body lasts forever,
Least of all the fathers, who hold their peace,
Who've shrunk to fit these astonishingly narrow beds.

And they keep the fathers in the hospitals
As if they'd turned up there like unclaimed luggage,
Never to be shipped to their proper address.

Oh, someday they'll make their ahistorical exits—
But not yet. So we watch them take their turns
For the worse, children wading out too far

Or climbing too tall a tree. Knowing no better,
They'll let us believe they once fed the earth,
That their lives were deliberate as money,

That soon we'll understand what makes them valuable.
Then they float off in smoky wreaths and condense,
Resettling on rooftops in a strange neighborhood;

No matter how we plead they won't climb down.

— STEVEN CRAMER

## The World Book

That night he came into my room,
The *World Book* tucked under his arm
(Volume 5, from *Desert* to *Electron*),

He pointed out the structure of my inner
Ear—the hammer, stirrup, and anvil,
The cross-sectioned spiral of the cochlea;

No matter how he diagrammed the ache,
He couldn't stop its throbbing. Years later
On the renal ward, I've brought in a Walkman

To help him pass the hours in dialysis.
His six quarts of blood have turned
Muddy red inside the yards of coiled tubing,

A tainted stream siphoned around a wheel
And through these artificial guts to surface
Purified. And my fantasy is childish:

I repair his faltering body, restitch the nets
Of capillaries, the membranes of hurt cells,
Or at least turn up an image to explain

What brought us here, one pair among twenty—
The patients becalmed and tethered to machines,
Pulsing shunts burrowed in their chests;

And stationed around them, the relatives,
Some motionless, some pacing, all keeping
Watch. My father's eyes close and tighten

As I hover above him. When he falls
Asleep, it's to a music I can't hear
And for which there is no metaphor.

— STEVEN CRAMER

## Father's Fall

The hospital lights punish my eyes.
A doctor is scolding me for not
considering my mother who does not
seem to have this problem
swallowing, keeping hiccups back,
keeping her dress dry. I will not
go upstairs to see him the doctor says,
I will sit here and stop it.

The police say he rolled
down the subway stairs. Blood
nests in his head like bad birds.
Upstairs they cut out
the crows. Something about
arithmetic, 50 and 50.

How could my daredevil father,
washer of Empire State windows,
91st floor, fall down 22 steps?

I think of the baby glass
in the kitchen. Afternoons
would fall into nights and his words
spin onto the table like aggies
until he could hardly
stand up to lie down.

Tonight, on the waiting-room couch
I lie in myself, awake and little.
*What if he dies here,*
*how will I get what I need?*—
hating my piggy heart.

— CAROLE SIMMONS OLES

## Simple Questions

*Can you hear me? Do you*
*understand?*

*How are you feeling? Can you*
*feel anything?*

*Are you in pain? Is there anything*
*I can do?*

*Do you know me? Do you*
*know who I am?*

    ★   ★   ★

When I dream about my father, he's
recovered. Home. He can move—walk; talk to
my mother; complain; even argue.
(The doctor at the hospital, not encouraging,
wouldn't deny this possibility.)

He comes downstairs and makes his way
toward his favorite chair, the one
with the florid cushions he'd stitched himself.
His breath comes hard, as it had
in the hospital; but suddenly, miraculously—

*better!*

I started having this dream
after my first visit.

    ★   ★   ★

"What comes after seven? Say it.
Try! What's the number after seven? . . . That's

right! Now what comes after eight? Tell me,
what comes after eight? . . ."
Once my mother got him to count
to fifteen.

Then, seven.

*    *    *

He was the old man you'd pass as you
hurried down the corridor to see your friend
in traction (touch football
terpsichore), or with pneumonia (not, thank God,
critical); the old man with the sucked-in
yellow face, no teeth, the oxygen tube
up his nose, the urine sac hanging from his bed.
Breathing hard; hardly moving; his eyes
blank, yet (weren't they?) following you . . .

Not your own.

The unhappy family whose
trouble he was . . .

NOT YOUR OWN.

*    *    *

"Hello! Say hello. How do you
feel? Are you feeling better?"

"A little better."

"Good." She leans over and
looks into his face. "Did you sleep OK?"

No answer.

"Do you know me? Who
am I? What's my name?"

"M-mom."

"And what's your name? Can you
tell me your name?"

"Sam."

"Good! Are you hungry? Let me give you
some soup? A little custard? . . ."

"No."

"Are you thirsty? Where's your straw?
Would you like some juice?"

"Yes."

"How about a nice shave? Would you
like me to give you a shave? . . . There!

"Now you look handsome!"

He rubs his face with his right hand;
he keeps rubbing his face.

\*   \*   \*

"Are you the son? What a pity! He seems like
such a nice person, such a sweet old man.
It's a shame . . . Last night he was very quiet—
slept like a baby. Didn't bother anybody!
By the end of the week he'll be ready to go home."

\*   \*   \*

"Wake up! Open your eyes. Can you
keep your eyes open?"

No answer.

"Look at me. Can you see me? Who
am I? Do you know who I am?"

No answer.

"Can you hear me? Do you understand
what I'm saying to you?"

". . . Yes."

"Look around. Where are you?
Do you know where you are?"

No answer.

"Can you feel anything? Can you feel
my hand? Where's my hand?"

I put my hand in his; he
squeezes hard.

"Who am I? Do you know who I am?"

". . . Yes."

"What's my name? Say it. Who
am I? Tell me who I am."

". . . Fa-ther."

\*　　\*　　\*

No love lost. A lifetime of
anger; resentment; disapproval. Could I pretend—
even now—a deep, personal concern?

Prodding him to speech (what the doctor
ordered), to recover enough of his mind to
help my mother endure his release,

hypnotized me, gripped my attention, the way
his right hand gripped my hand—the last remnant
of his unrelenting, fist-clenched

denunciations of the world:

of the "Hitler Brothers," who refused him even
a moment's rest in the sweatshops where he
spent his working life stitching men's clothes;

of relatives, or neighbors, never generous or
grateful enough, for someone rarely generous
or grateful; of my friends, of *me*—stymied by my

anger; resentment; disapproval . . . The way
his right hand gripped the hedgecutter, lifted it,
and aimed it at my head.

"I have to go now. Goodbye! I'll see you
tomorrow . . . Do you hear me?
Feel better. I hope you feel better."

\*     \*     \*

"How do you feel? Talk to me. Tell me
how you feel."

". . . Not so good."

"Are you in pain? Where does
it hurt you?"

No answer.

"Can I do anything? Should I
get the doctor?"

". . . No doctor can cure me."

\*    \*    \*

"He had a restless night, couldn't swallow—we had to pump out his
throat. His pressure
sank way down. There was nothing else we
could do . . . I'm sorry. He just fell
asleep, very peaceful, and stopped breathing."

\*    \*    \*

"Can you hear me?"
"Yes."

"How are you feeling?"
"A little better."

"Do you know me? Who am I?"
"My son."

"Is there anything I can do?"
"No."

— LLOYD SCHWARTZ

## My Mother's Stroke

Your right eye goes blank,
Can't see even the dark.
The dog barks, and you hear
No bark.

Messages your brain sends
Down your left side, derailed,
Never get where they're going,
and the slow slide

Of your whole brain
Is like that of that train
to Southend—
Went straight off at the bend, didn't it,

And into the lake.
But you can still make
The odd, small gesture,
That thought-out investiture

Of movement with sense,
And in your mind, you dance
Under the lake. The puff-fish, the pancake,
Even the devilfish trailing his whispery wake

Nod and bow
As you waltz underwater.
The music bubbles to the surface and me,
Your wondering, admiring, loving, listening daughter.

— KELLY CHERRY

## Upon My Mother's Death

Skull in the mirror, nodding: I can cope.
The dance of numbness and despair and hope.
Spring in the window beckoning escape.

Flail for an answer with the grin intact.
The ravaged body in the bath: a fact.
Grim vistas part like clouds to bare the act.

Mesmeric, these perspectives of the end:
the dying mother and the helpless friend
who is not dying, or so I pretend.

Black barbell balanced into slow May green,
two struggles with a city in between.
I walk upright, the chaos clamped within.

Monday. Hospital balcony.
Man smoking—gaunt, pajamaed, with IV.
His neighbor smiles, a chubby amputee.

Tuesday. Sunset reddens every tree.
Down in the park a black dog is at play,
perfect and tiny, seen as from the sky.

Wednesday. I bring Italian ice—too late.
You have already left. You couldn't wait
after the silent summons to the gate.

Encountering your death took all this time!
I've finally reached it. At that very same
second you vanished, having left your name.

Handbag and glasses, paperbacks and shoes,
the pristine toothpaste that you never used:
these may not be the relics I would choose,

but wait. Condition supersedes event.
Serenity spreads over the lament,
legacy given, message fully meant.

I and my cousin at the "chapel" door
(Thursday) turn to look at you once more—
never to forget you as you were?

Pale and composed, not solemn but severe,
you are already absent; also here.
We kiss your forehead, touch your cold white hair.

Outside, the boulevard of afternoon.
Bursts of rhythm, summer's jagged tune,
embrace of heat that dissipates too soon.

Yet underneath the hubbub things feel still.
Knowledge unspoken. The undaunted will.
The waiting countryside. And love's deep well.

— RACHEL HADAS

## The Selfishness of the Sick

The selfishness of the sick is enviable.
They can have anything they want,
they think, and so they make demands.

All is forgiven in the caves
no one else wants to enter.
They are bathed by strangers,
gently held while their pillows
are fluffed and rearranged. They
are served all of their meals and get
exactly what they ask for.

They eat, they drink, they drowse
on so much love, on painkillers,
dreaming of the old world
where they can
walk to what they want, unassisted.

— BETH JOSELOW

## Blue Baby

Sister of the congenital heart, meant to be
two years younger than I,
playmate for swings and dolls.
You, Patricia, doll of my parents'
love nights, there was no time—blue death
staining lips and fingertips, creeping
toward the murmur in your nursery crib.

Without you, I grew, whispered to your shadow,
played sister to our dolls—
and saw you often, deep
in the garden of our mother's eyes.
Still I bloomed, forgot you
until my guilt matured: a blue vein
that twists now in the pulse of my heart.

— JUDITH MINTY

## Stroke

After the family dinner, language
is trivial and easy—
until you lose it entirely, Uncle,
asking for something you want
which suddenly has no name.
"Goddamn," you moan, "gimme a . . .
All I want's a . . . Jesus Christ,
ain't you got one?"
The family hands you sweaters,
pills, icepicks, glasses of brandy,
knives. Nothing will do.
Afraid of empty hands,
they rush at you with objects,
determined to interpret what you've said,
afraid to name this dying
and to watch you leave them, word by word.

— SUSAN IRENE REA

## Fever Wit

If a child or young adult lay
near crisis with a temperature,
bedclothes hot as from an iron,
face swollen bright as a blown coal,
neighbors and kin would gather round,
sitting near the bedside leaning
close, awaiting words uttered from
delirium, the scattered phrase
and mutter from hot throat and brain.
Every mumble seemed a message
to interpret, each groan and wince,
jerk and whisper, a report in
testimony from other tongues,
as though the sick child glowing with
infection could see beyond in
fever intoxication, become
a filament for lighting their
ordinary lives with lightning glimpse
burned through the secret boundary,
the ill one privileged to say
across and not distort or resist
the wisdom of sickness, the vision
from pain-fire's further peaks, before
the dreaded sweat, the chill descent.

— ROBERT MORGAN

## The Glass

I think of it with wonder now,
the glass of mucus that stood on the table
next to my father all weekend. The cancer is
growing fast in his throat now,
and as it grows it sends out pus like the
sun sending out solar flares, those
pouring tongues of fire. So my father has to
gargle, hack, cough, and spit a
mouth full of thick stuff
into the glass every ten minutes or so,
scraping the glass up his lower lip to
get the last bit off his skin, then he
sets the glass down on the table and it
sits there, shiny and faintly
gold like a glass of beer foam, he
gurgles and reaches for it again and
gets the heavy sputum out,
full of bubbles and moving around like yeast—he is
like some god producing dark food from his own mouth.
He himself can eat nothing anymore,
just a swallow of milk sometimes,
cut with water, and even then it
can't always get past the tumor,
and the next time the saliva comes up it's
chalkish and ropey, he has to roll it a
long time in his throat like a ball of
clay to form it and get it up and dis-
gorge the elliptical globule into the cup—
and the wonder to me is that it did not disgust me,
that glass of phlegm that stood there all day and
filled slowly with compound globes and then I'd
empty it and it would fill again and
shimmer there on the table until the
room seemed to turn around it

in an orderly way, like a model of the solar system
turning around the gold sun,
my father like the dark earth that
used to be the center of the universe, now
turning with the rest of us
around his death—bright glass of
spit on the table, these last mouthfuls of his life.

— SHARON OLDS

## The Moment of My Father's Death

When he breathed his last breath it was he,
my father, although he was so transformed
no one who had not been with him
for the last hours would know him, the gold
skin luminous as cold animal fat,
the eyes cast all the way back into his head,
the whites gleaming like a white iris, the
nose that grew thinner and thinner every minute, the
open mouth racked open with that
tongue in it like all the heartbreak of the mortal,
a tongue so dried, scalloped, darkened and
material. You could see the mucus
risen like gorge into the back of his mouth
but it was he, the huge slack yellow arms,
the spots of blood under the skin
black and precise, we had come this far with him
step by step, it was he, his last
breath was his, not taken with desire but
his, light as the sphere of a dandelion seed
coming out of his mouth and floating across the room.
Then the nurse pulled up his gown and
listened for his heart, I saw the stomach
silvery and hairy, it was his stomach, she
moved to the foot of the bed and stood there, she
did not shake her head she stood and
nodded at me. And for a minute it was fully
he, my father, dead but completely
himself, a man with an open mouth and
no breath, gold skin and
black spots on his arms, I kissed him and
spoke to him. He looked like someone
killed in a violent bloodless struggle, all that
strain in his neck, that look of pulling back, that
stillness he seemed to be holding at first and

then it was holding him, the skin
tightened slightly around his whole body
as if the purely physical were claiming him,
and then it was not my father,
it was not a man, it was not an animal, I
stood and ran my hand through the silver hair,
plunged my fingers into it gently and
lifted them up slowly through the grey
waves of it, the unliving glistening
matter of this world.

— SHARON OLDS

## Last Elegy

Surgeons cutting a hole
in my father's skull
with one of those saws that lift
a plug out of bone also took
a big lump off my spine
in the dream I don't understand
that flickered back
the day before he died.
We were at the shore following
a golf match on TV,
eating, napping. His drained
gray face didn't reveal
any sense of being here,
any desire to live.
The money he made,
the failure he thought he was
in love, in business,
intensified his mood
after the heart attack.
The sky blew flat, smeary gray,
a few fly-like figures
paced the cold beach. Millie,
Clair, Margot, Mom and I
didn't know how to stop his
staring out of nothing into nothing,
so we watched hard
Nicklaus miss two easy putts
and other famous pros tee off
with that quick fluid swing
they have, then stroll down
the fairway to the ball,
the whole world manicured, green.
To say, "I love you"
meant "I know I'm dying,"

but you said it,
at least I think I heard you
whisper it to me. Or was it to yourself?
I kept my eyes on the screen.

— STEPHEN BERG

## Cells

My father, climbing stairs in tenements
to visit his parolees, frightened, a gun
in his holster he knew he'd never shoot.
Two hours a day packed into a subway.
Thirty years. Almost a life sentence.

My father, 74, incarcerated on the 14th
floor of a vast teaching hospital,
wearing striped pajamas and hooked
to a machine lit up like something
you drop quarters into. He raises
his head weakly and whispers,
*P.J. you have a real hepatitis face.*

*Intensive Care:* My mother, bending
over the bed, one of the tubes
sustaining him, blood and potassium
dripping in, maintaining
a proper electrolyte balance.

I'm leaving, riding back to Boston
on an old Pennsylvania Railroad car.
The air in here is greasy, poisonous.
We pass the Connecticut Sound. Three
bathers, heads teetering on a platter
of scummy water. A billboard
with this graffiti: *Rosie, I Love You.*

The word love, read in a jolt of wheels.
Astonishing. Ineludible. Like a blissful
couple, joined at the chest, thighs,
knees, kissing in the doorway
you're trying to exit through.

— PHYLLIS JANOWITZ

## Heart Failures

My dear, you described it
in such clear detail I should have seen
for myself, suspected from the start.
  You know how we are, though,
all of us (even yourself, surely?),
about these things: reality comes hard
  and never fast enough
to be the rule . . . I suppose the rain
distracted me, the storm in the air
  but not yet upon us.
Still, just your tone must have meant *something*
at that point—the really awful part
  when your father drove you
all those flat miles out to the new farm
(your voice faltered then), arriving there
  with the rain that came down
soon like dye, darkening everything.
You watched him run, hunched and determined
  between the black puddles
to an ominous haystack, and then
it happened, silent in the blurred lens
  of the Packard windshield:
as if he *meant* to, sliding slowly
into the mud. You had never heard
  of a coronary,
and when he cursed you back to the car
you obeyed, of course. What could you do
  but peer through the downpour
while his limbs twitched, and a kind of mist
—the emanation of pain, it was—
  aureoled his body
where it lay in the rain another
hour until a neighbor took you both
  away. Remembering
how you turned into a child again,

just telling it, *his* witnessing child,
   I guess who I am, too
(it was all so simple, once you set
the scene), lying here awake, lying
   with what is left of you
cold in the sheets against me. The rain
hisses under traffic—it has come
   for good then, so to speak.
I know who I am *for you.* I know,
suffering my private spasm here,
   how anonymously
you yielded when I caught your long legs
in mine: not yours, not mine. From how far
   you must have been staring
through what dim glass, while my foreign nerves
performed! I know who I am—who cares?
   It is as true of this
seizure as of that other: *having*
teaches us little, nothing of love
   whose presence we locate,
and whose power, only in our losses.
You stir in my arms and say, "I thought
   the rain would never come."
Now that it has, my dear, I almost
fear that it will never end. Never.

— RICHARD HOWARD

## Sugar

He was three years old
and growing smaller.
Seven hours in a coma
while the nurses probed
his tense, white skin,
till the silvery life
of electrolytes and insulin
kicked in.
      He'll make it.
I asked for a Valium
and stepped outside
where the question moon
suggested vertigo
beyond blood numbers,
digital, a wind
beyond those cubicles
of artificial light.
Diabetes Mellitus.
We'll make it.
Breathe it in,
the doctor said without apology,
put it in your lungs.

      We moved
around some, got adjusted.
Fragrant autumn nights
he leaves the back door open.
He says he likes
the way it looks
to let the outside in,
to see nothing but
the glow-in-the-dark
astronaut poster
and the luminous earth
from where he falls

gracefully through space.
Isn't it beautiful, he says,
to be *almost* blind.
And he's fine now,
I can say it; even when
I touch his eleven year old
needle-toughened skin,
I only feel my *own*
fear.

      It's me
who's growing smaller,
wondering how he sees
me by day
as he drifts slowly
down the hill alone
on his way to school,
waving to me
as though my face
were the earth,
and he the luminous astronaut
floating beyond
the gravity of home.

— BARBARA ANDERSON

## Talking to Grief

Ah, grief, I should not treat you
like a homeless dog
who comes to the back door
for a crust, for a meatless bone.
I should trust you.

I should coax you
into the house and give you
your own corner,
a worn mat to lie on,
your own water dish.

You think I don't know you've been living
under my porch.
You long for your real place to be readied
before winter comes. You need
your name,
your collar and tag. You need
the right to warn off intruders,
to consider
my house your own
and me your person
and yourself
my own dog.

— DENISE LEVERTOV

## Hearing with My Son

> *Our studies show that the autistic child apparently has a*
> *random relationship with sounds, linking them with whatever*
> *object holds his attention at the moment.*

Crouched by his chair, my son hears
my complaint from the wine glass,
my praise from his own shoe.
When I read him books, I speak
through their pictures, or the wall.

Despite my love, I say less and less—
even if he heard me in the trees
or the sunset, he would not listen.

Perhaps, somewhere on the soft and hot
savannahs of Kenya, a newborn gazelle
speaks with the voice of my son.

He throws his cup across the room.
His hand explodes with the crash.

— STEPHEN COREY

## The Return: Intensive Care

I felt for the button . . .
There's a circle of perpetual occultation
at the depressed pole,
within which stars never rise,
and, at the elevated one, one of apparition,
from which they never fall.
I used these facts
to figure the limits of my situation
—mine? or was it yours?—
as again I came back.

Where was I?
I thumbed the button for your floor.
It lit.
Suddenly, I thought,
everywhere there are circles,
as in some new weather or fashion:
the breasts both of a young farm girl
and, sadder, of a fat old orderly
riding up beside me;
the elevator's orbicular lamp bulbs;

and colored like linen,
each drop of snow the night before,
big and round as a saucer—
a night such as we persist in
calling a freak, though it isn't
anything more than the cycling back of things
too cursedly familiar.
Yes, though it was spring,
though it was April,
the moon had worn a great wet halo.

Signifying what?
Why look up

the facts on charts?
How often in history
has everything happened!
The nurse again wheeled away
your tray with its apple, untouched,
and two dark plums,
which precisely matched,
in color and conformation,

the raccoon rounds
of valor and exhaustion
through which your eyes peered,
brighter, still, than any planet.
*O Jesus Jesus Jesus Jesus Jesus!*
Inwardly I cried,
to me the word
recurring like any old habit.
Poor stately Jew, forgive the helplessness
that enforced my genteel outward mode

as you lay there,
my small-talk Yankee palaver
of mercilessness in Mother Nature—
buds in remission,
pathetic birds
spiralling up from the sheeted roads
as if, I surmised, nothing now remained
but vertical migration.
I dropped my eyes. All else, anything
that I might have been moved to say,

anything that might have reached to the heart
of what we may or may not be
here on earth
to do or serve, dismayed
and frightened me.
O David, I couldn't speak

of anything beyond the trivial,
by horror of risk held back,
by horror of saying something
even more banal.

You were on morphine.
You who for the length of this evil illness
had never complained
but had made of yourself a figure—
*Look to the light,*
or *Don't try to cling...*
Shy of prayer,
desperate with my own feckless
impulse to speech, at length I hung
as if in midair

as the dark outside
began again its round.
All so cursedly dignified!
At length, in the distilled absence of sound,
I recalled my *why why why why why!*
at the death of my small terrier.
What a petty thing to remember!
And yet perhaps those yelps
when I was so young
were the only eloquence possible.

As was perhaps the gentle rejoinder
(she had seen more than I)
of my mother's mother:
*Revelation helps.*
There in the hospital,
lacking for words to tender,
I had recourse to fashion.
Forgive me, I nattered;
then left, once more depressing the button;
then lifted my eyes,

searching a sign of perpetuation.
Would it do any good to tell you that I cried?
There were stars, or there were none,
from wherever it was I stood.
There was, or there wasn't, a moon.

— SYDNEY LEA

## Angina

That one who is the dreamer lies mostly in her left arm,
Where the pain shows first,
Tuned in on the inmost heart,
Never escaping. On the blue, bodied mound of chenille,
That limb lies still.
Death in the heart must be calm,

Must not look suddenly, but catch the window-framed squirrel
In a mild blue corner
Of an eye staring straight at the ceiling
And hold him there.
Cornered also, the oak tree moves
All the ruffled green way toward itself

Around the squirrel thinking of the sun
As small boys and girls tiptoe in
Overawed by their existence,
For courtly doctors long dead
Have told her that to bear children
Was to die, and they are the healthy issue

Of four of those. Oh, beside that room the oak leaves
Burn out their green in an instant, renew it all
From the roots when the wind stops.
All afternoon she dreams of letters
To disc jockeys, requesting the "old songs,"
The songs of the nineties, when she married, and caught

With her first child rheumatic fever.
Existence is family: sometime,
Inadequate ghosts round the bed,
But mostly voices, low voices of serious drunkards
Coming in with the night light on
And the pink radio turned down;

She hears them ruin themselves
On the rain-weeping wires, the bearing-everything poles,
Then dozes, not knowing sleeping from dying—
It is day. Limbs stiffen when the heart beats
Wrongly. Her left arm tingles,
The squirrel's eye blazes up, the telephone rings,

Her children and her children's children fail
In school, marriage, abstinence, business.
But when I think of love
With the best of myself—that odd power—
I think of riding, by chairlift,
Up a staircase burning with dust

In the afternoon sun slanted also
Like stairs without steps
To a room where an old woman lies
Who can stand on her own two feet
Only six strange hours every month:
Where such a still one lies smiling

And takes her appalling risks
In absolute calm, helped only by the most
Helplessly bad music in the world, where death,
A chastened, respectful presence
Forced by years of excessive quiet
To be stiller than wallpaper roses,

Waits, twined in the roses, saying slowly
To itself, as sprier and sprier
Generations of disc jockeys chatter,
I must be still and not worry,
Not worry, not worry, to hold
My peace, my poor place, my own.

— JAMES DICKEY

## Intensive Care

In the antiseptic Eden,
your small light burns:
a green dot
that carried you
across two continents,
from coal-mining village,
cricket for the county,
and Oxford ribbons,
to picturesque America,
where life is a bonfire
and a man's heart
does not attack him.

For fourteen years
I've huddled close
to that heart
strangers decode
by echo-scan
and oscilloscope.
The smocked magicians
of rhythm
turn level eyes
to your pounding
electricity.

Midnight.
All our totemic animals
are asleep:
the kangaroos,
the panther,
the harvest mouse,
the camel,
the prairie dogs,
the lion:

the full bestiary
of our animal love.
The doctors, your mother,
and your poet all asleep.
Only your heart
lies awake.

With ink and a stylus
it scratches out
a story,
speaking its dialect
all quiver and pump.
You may sleep,
but the novelist
in your chest
never sleeps,
minting yarns
bold, stylish, and macabre.

When it gabbles,
alarms ring
up and down the ward.
"Are you all right?"
a nurse wakes you to ask,
and you know your heart
has been rambling again
while you slept,
slipping off the hoods
and turning all
its falcons loose.

At home alone
across the lake,
a darkness too possible
invades the house
and my chest becomes

a suit of armor
shrunk tight by worry.
Mi casa es su casa.

I want to fly
to that ward
black as a mine shaft
where you drowse,
thatched deep
in wire and electrode,
still gamely
performing
a ventriloquism
from the heart:
on a monitor
your small light
glowing like radium.

— DIANE ACKERMAN

## For a Friend in the Hospital

On the way to visit you the other day,
I passed a colony of dandelions
bunched up against the corner of a building,
and I knew you would have seen them
as persecuted weeds, exiled from the field,
huddled together under that brick wall.

I love the idea of flowers "escaping
from cultivation," as the field guides say,
and becoming wild again, but these
had come together to create
their own garden in the hard clay.
And I knew you would have loved them for that

and picked one, perhaps, drinking the sour milk
through the straw of its green stem.

— JEFFREY HARRISON

## Moonrise as Abstraction

Last night, driving west along the parkway
toward the hospital, he watched the old moon
lift itself once more above the treeline.

The oncoming lights blurred large & ominous,
whirred past, then curved away. Bare branches
stretched their fingers upward, black etched black

against the silver black. He saw the pockmarked
craters of the old moon's eyes stare past him
and knew then that his friend was dying.

There was a grinding in the going round of wheels
as the lights rushed up to meet him.
Except for the preternatural brilliance

of the eyes, his friend would be a shadow only,
the waning of a light which for a time
had blotted out the other lights around,

a light egyptian, regal, unlike the common string
of traffic lights approaching, and for
a while still closer than the cold & distant stars.

In the darkened room on the sixth floor
of the hospital, he would watch his friend's eyes
fixed upon the game, as if the outcome mattered

anymore, when what mattered was that where
his friend was going he could not follow,
though he'd prayed to keep him from this final

journey west. Then, as the wheels beneath him
rounded one more bend, he looked up
to see the moon shake the treeline free

like the solitary king it is, and he felt
his fist unclenching as he bid goodbye, as if
at last his friend might ease him on his way.

— PAUL MARIANI

## On Tuesdays They Open the
## Local Pool to the Stroke Victims

FOR MY SONS

Thank God my own father didn't have to go through this.
Or I'd be driving him here every Tuesday
So he could swim his laps
Or splash around with the others
In the shallow end. Something terrible
Has been bled out of these lives. Why else
Would they be here pulling themselves along on their sides,
Scissoring, having to prove to their middle-aged sons
They can still dance.
                          The last three days I heard water
In the cellar, the rooms below me bumping together
Like dingies. Somewhere back in my sleep
My father splashes in the shallow end.
All these men, even
The balding ones waiting behind the chain-link fence
Watching their fathers, are down there
At the bottom of the stairs.
They are all gliding like sunlight,
Like trout across the cold floors of their breeding ponds.

— ROBERT HEDIN

## Her Stroke

Even a lover is always, forever,
outside the grip of that gravity
where mother and daughter
interlock. Here she's slipping, on
and back: you clasp at her
as I hover near.
               I can't
know her, now. There's no time.
Smell of camphor, dust of bromide.
The bed stanchioned with perpendicular
silver rods. The woman we watch there
is not like you; physical echoes,
but all her extensions tied up
and abstracted. The tongue frays
at the edge of the sentence,
the fingers at the hem of the sheet.
I try to imagine the dancer she was,
hot as sunlight criss-crossed
in a handglass.
                 You're impatient—
even angry. I haven't seen, not
exactly. She was elegant and sharp.
  It's not that she's changed
through shadings, like weather
                     but actually
vanished, only halfway returned.

Whatever your fury, you couldn't
have known. Who ever expects
treachery? faults
in the bloodstream, pulse
shut down
           for seconds
while the body is paralyzed, waiting,
  as arteries seize on a dot

the heart had forgotten.
You say
maybe this is not your mother
but someone else, to be cared for
differently.
    Fear, and exhaustion.
Yet so much of what was
is still clear, in what you do—
your voices, your hair—the ways
you both motion toward the blossoms
in the jar. I love her as I would love
someone wounded. You love her
for everything, everything
you are.

— JIM SCHLEY

## Nursing Home

My mother babbles. A salad of noises.
'You know who this is?' asks my aunt and I dread
some horror of an answer, but no,
nothing. She rubs her tray instead.
'It's clean,' says my aunt, 'the tray is clean.
Evelyn, what are you cleaning? Play
with your cards, play *pishy-posh*,' and then she
laughs, that overflowing, tilts
her head at the word and laughs who sits
all day in her chair with her cards in a sweater
embroidered with flowers, all day each day
where the t.v. flickers. My aunt thinks she chose
senility. My aunt says you have to keep
moving, never worry, avoid
abiding mourning,
things that refuse to change.

— BARRY SPACKS

## Let Me In

What goes on inside those ambulance boxes,
those little worlds of activity negotiating the traffic?
I've always been awkward about pulling to the side,
wedging myself between a pillar of the El
and a van, or too slow to take the shoulder.
For three minutes the ambulance wailed
my grandmother to the hospital less than three blocks away
but across and around the parkway.
"Oy vey" she gasped, fell back
on her bed and became so light my mother
could move her. The year before when she'd fallen
on the way to the bathroom and broken
her ribs, she was impossible to move,
her thick legs splayed, the ulcerous flesh,
the heavy breasts still alive.
But oy vey, and that was it, except
for a technicality machines sustained.
That day my period had come, I was trying
to conceive, and the failure became dating
of the pregnancy I did have.
It wasn't a girl I could name for her
but somehow he was her, somehow, her still there.
The laugh, this boy's clear blue eyes—
they're hers. At least I can believe so.
The ambulance couldn't do anything for her.
Still they go past now, in every one a little story,
a little store window of pain,
there they go, taking someone, no her, her, her.
I pull over, I want to follow them this time,
this time it's her. That's where she's gone, it's her. Let me in.

— JUDITH BAUMEL

## The Night Grandma Died

Adrift on the pillows. "She just died," said the nurse.
"A heart attack," the doctor said.
"It was easy, peaceful," I told her daughter.

I tried to picture the pincers of heaven
reaching down and twitching her, a little wrinkled diamond,
from the sweet white cot she lay on.

Tears and sniffles. My consolation
didn't work. Not even for me.
What was it, in the end, that wouldn't go away?

The bed. The feel of the cold rails
sliding up and down when people came with needles,
the gray rails grating, clanking, her fingers

yearning toward them like a baby's lips,
hoping for suction. And the white sheets
stiff as sails, scraping skin as if skin were wind, insubstantial.
And the night light, flashing, going out, flashing again.
And the tough mattress, sullen as a shark's back,
rising toward the nurse's hands

on its steel track.

— SANDRA GILBERT

## The Orchid

What do you remember of me?
The last time I saw you alive you had grown
white as the hospital sheet,
a pale orchid under the oxygen tent,
strange greenhouse.

Grandma, today I saw people on television
who had been revived from death.
They told how they rose
out of their bodies and saw operating rooms,
doctors hovering above white tables.
Others saw their bodies asleep in bed
and roamed their houses as naturally
as they had in life.
Could you see me standing by your shoulder
flower like a crucifix in my hand?

Describe that face for me,
the eyes that saw the orchid bloom.

— DAVID BOTTOMS

## Counting

An oriental ink drawing:
a shadowy range of mountains,
and a gray lake rising. Pneumonia
is the name of the country on the lighted screen,
the chest of my two-year-old daughter.

                                         At home
in her pink eggshell room,
I dig blindly in drawers for clothes,
and for something familiar and comforting
to take her at the hospital.
My fingers are caught in a string of beads,
the rosary my mother
has had the priest bless for my child's birthday:
"Teach her to count on Christ," instructed
the accompanying card.

                              A disbeliever
in the power of objects, I allow this penitent's jewelry,
the chain of linked sets of beads,
to slip through my fingers, joining my hands
into the steeple of an unsteady temple.
The part of my brain
I never listen to any more begins
a litany of prayers in my mother's voice. I hear
myself joining in, counting down deep enough
to where I can believe
that beads of amber glass can be magical.

— JUDITH ORTIZ COFER

## Now, before the End, I Think

Now, before the end, I think
of how it was when we began:
in holding hands before we knew
each other, in touch there was the silent
awe of what we soon would know
in knowing one another later,
as though to heal the wounds that words
would cause before they were inflicted.

Now, wordless again, you reach to hold
my hand as if to say in silence,
it is healed, we touch, we are together.
We have heard the end, drifting
to the brink of a new silence,
holding hands in awe of being
now together, this moment, now,
now before we part forever.

— EDWIN HONIG

## Frank Amos and the Way Things Work

My wife and I are standing in my sister's yard,
    talking to the man who built our house,
    across the field from here. He's retired now,

though he looks much as he did eight years ago,
    when horses grazed our hill. But he's not well;
    we've known for about a year. We ask him how it's going.

"Not too bad. They do this radiation"—
    he pronounces the first *a* short—"every two weeks,
    ten treatments. I've got these maps on my chest, see"—

he opens his shirt, and there the purple crosses
    and rectangles are. "Got 'em like that on my back, too.
    The lens that shoots the rays is up overhead,

and there's a big dish, like, underneath—maybe
    to catch the rays after they've gone through me,
    I don't know. The lens and dish are hung

to a big circular rack that they can rotate
    around the table, so you don't have to move
    when they want to shoot from the other side.

I told 'em today, my breast bone sticks out
    too much or something, I can't lie down too long
    on this hard table, so I'll just hold myself up

on my arms till you tell me I have to lie down
    and hold still. Seemed to go all right.
    I have to go all the way to Winchester

for the treatments—five minutes. Down here,
    all they have is a CAT scan. See one of those?
    You should. They run you through it and stop you

every inch or so, and it takes a picture
    just like you'd been sliced in two. Cross section."
    A grasshopper jumps against my leg; I think

of the day the inside framing got to where
    he could see how the walls would be, and he said,
    "God, this'll be a bitch of a sheetrock job."

He leans against the van, eyes bright, the last
    two letters of his CB handle—GRAYBEARD—
    emerging from behind him. "I don't know,

I just have a feeling, I think we're going
    to come out of this all right." We pass the evening
    talking over things you have to imagine

with your hands, taking turns with the pleasure
    of being understood, touching on work in the West
    Virginia coal mines, black blasting powder, the way

one man on a bridge-building crew would toss
    hot rivets with a pair of tongs and the man
    on the girder would catch them in this tin thing,

like a funnel, and then we get on carbide lanterns—
    back to the mines—and from there to the old-time
    gas lights fed by acetylene produced

in a carbide plant you built outside, just far
    enough from the house, because every so often
    a batch of carbide would explode, and you

didn't want anything like that in the cellar.
    Better to have it off a little ways.
    And all the time part of me is watching him,

wondering how sick he is, thinking *This
is the man who built our house.* Finally
it's past supper time, and he takes off.

We wish him the best, and send regards to Myrtle,
and the old van backs into the turnaround
and lurches toward the road. The rest of us

go inside to my sister's kitchen, and look out
in time to see him coming back. He leans out his window.
"Henry, I don't know why I didn't remember

till I got out to the road, but it's just come to me—
the town lights over in Romney used to run
on carbide, like we were talking about.

They had a big plant that put out enough gas
to do all the street lights. I just happened
to remember that, and I thought you'd like to know."

— HENRY TAYLOR

## Parents Support Group

Our children half-lost, we gather at the table,
Making small polite jokes
About weather and coffee. The blinds are drawn.
Outside, the summer afternoon is tennis strokes,

A grackle calling to its mate, wind-chimes,
Sliding tailgates of delivery vans. Long-timers smile
And pat the new arrivals' backs. Our therapist
Takes a long, long, long, long, *long* while

Before he starts, reluctantly. That hot potato, Pain,
Goes round and round the table. Who of us
Are blameless, who share blame
For why our children left a crust

Of blood across their wrists, gulped pills, or think
Their terribly thin bodies still are fat,
Did drugs, did drink
Behind ripped billboards of their raw self-hate?

We don't know. Weeks . . . or was it days ago,
Self-tucked in the illusion we control
Our lives . . . sane, in our accepting this . . . we thought
That all stones roll

Downhill, all rabbits leap, the months ahead
Are simply spaces on our calendars
Where plans are penciled or not penciled in.
That's normal and not wrong . . . But now we're here

Talking with strangers. To our left
The lady in a green dress weeps; the man
Whose daughter must be begged or bribed to eat
Keeps putting up and putting down his hand,

Then polishing his glasses on his paisley tie.
I don't know what to say. I don't know anything
That can help us all. Words alone
(How many words there were!) have come unstrung

And scatter everywhere. Back in their halls
Our children hunch above their Scrabble board,
Or shoot the breeze
As aimlessly as they shot down our world.

— DICK ALLEN

# Women:
## Flowers of Ether in My Hair

## Maternity

when they checked me in, i was thinking: *this is going to be
a snap!* but at the same time, everything looked so different!
this was another world, ordered and white. the night moved
by on wheels.

suddenly the newness of the bed, the room, the quiet,
the hospital gown they put me in, the sheets rolled up
hard and starched and white and everything white except the
clock on the wall in red and black and the nurse's back as
she moved out of the room without speaking, everything
conspired to make me feel afraid.

*how long, how much will i suffer?*

the night looked in from bottomless windows.

— TOI DERRICOTTE

## The Presentation

they wheeled her out of the delivery room on a silver cart,
a piece of limp meat without a soul. when she woke the
day was fine crystal filaments shaking itself around
her.

she waited for something wrapped like a package, something
that knew its name better than she knew it; a thing she
had to discover, to unwrap and count, slowly, parting the
visible.

under her gown, the body of a stranger fed itself, sucked
moisture into her breasts, collapsed her womb like dried
eggplant.

a new muscle shaped her, clamped itself over her being.
whatever was left, hung limp: a dumb creature, numbly
attending.

— TOI DERRICOTTE

## A Valediction in the Waiting Room

Never in that summer of my first
muscular kiss, my chin rubbed rough
by his, as I stumbled past the kitchen's
tiny night-light to my room to roll
in pleasure all my own, would I have dreamed
of this. Although my Aunt Irene prayed
and prayed for children, none came. But what
did I know of that? She slid back on the slats
of an Adirondack chair, her eyes half-closed,
while my sisters and I swam and dripped and hopped
on hot feet around her on the beach.
It's almost summer now, but here I sit—

a washout in fluorescent light, joined
by my husband, whose hair, when combed just so
across his crown, can make a hopeful ghost
at most. *Childless,* my Aunt Irene. But now
*Child-free* is the phrase whose high gloss denies
loss, yet if savored long enough
releases its essence of restless emptiness.
Oh women! Remember the long, bare beach
just barely lit, just you and him and the dog
you'd loved almost a decade long damp
and happy? Now I can't count the times
I've watched my husband hold up tiny vials
in white light, squeeze the dropper, watch
his watch, then let the tremulous drop drop
as we held our breath. . . . Certain words are not
spoken here. Her hands on my belly, her face
turned from mine, the doctor pressed my uterus
as if to seal a stubborn envelope,
pronounced me *healed, contracted, closed.* Although
they were a thousand miles away, I know
my sisters sat together and know what words
tumbled onto the table between them, *lost*

*the baby,* the kitchen windows wild with snow
speeding up, coming down. By spring

it was time to try again. Again I tried
and tried and tried, like a manic comic
who slams herself against a wall, slams
and falls. Sometimes when this room's crammed
with silence and one more couple's coming
through the door, I'm edgy as a car-alarm,
about to yelp—too late! too late! But who
will listen? Not women who fly from three
adjacent states to see this specialist,
sun scanning each plane as it circles
in the air. Like me, like us, they know
about the clock that ticks, tolls, the river
that rolls below the hills behind the houses
where we lived as girls. What would I say
to my mother if she came banging at this door,
*What's taking you so long?* who bloomed and bore
six times without a thought? Or Aunt Irene,
still saying her rosary, praying down
to the bud of His body for my ovaries,
uterus? Or to the one I was,
—still leggy, high-hipped, who still had time to slip
off into summer streets where boys, stripped
to the waist, leaned against gleaming cars and swapped
the details of fantastic accidents.

— DEBRA BRUCE

## Once in Ohio

I would have done
    almost anything
Not to have had to
    see her joining me
That first time in
    the claw-footed tub
In Athens, her robe
    falling and a long
Red welt, the kind
    a bicycle chain
Can make, bristling over
    the ribs, the left
Side of her chest.
    She stood there,
And I could make out
    past her, drifting
Through the chute of light
    at the window, clusters
Of snowflakes like scraps
    of paper from a bonfire,
Lifted by their burning
    and then released.
I knew that everything
    had been changed,
And I was afraid, I was
    like a cedar fitted
For the winter with snow;
    and then she started to
Step in, and I helped her
    sit down facing me
As the warm water rose
    around us both.

— ARTHUR SMITH

## What Was Lost

What fed my daughters, my son
Trickles of bliss,
My right guess, my true information,
What my husband sucked on
For decades, so that I thought
Myself safe, I thought love
Protected the breast.

What I admired myself, liking
To leave it naked, what I could
Soap and fondle in its bath, what tasted
The drunken airs of summer like a bear
Pawing a hive, half up a sycamore.
I'd let sun eyeball it, surf and lakewater
Reel wildly around it, the perfect fit,
The burst of praise. Lifting my chin
I'd stretch my arms to point it at people,
Show it off when I danced. I believed this pride
Would protect it, it was a kind of joke
Between me and my husband
When he licked off some colostrum
Even a drop or two of bitter milk.
He'd say *You're saving for your grandchildren.*

I was doing that, and I was saving
The goodness of it for some crucial need,
The way a woman
Undoes her dress to feed
A stranger, at the end of *The Grapes of Wrath*,
A book my mother read me when I was
Spotty with measles, years before
The breast was born, but I remembered it.
How funny I thought goodness would protect it.
Jug of star fluid, breakable cup—

Someone shoveled your good and bad crumbs
Together into a plastic container
Like wet sand at the beach,
For breast tissue is like silicon.
And I imagined inland orange groves,
Each tree standing afire with solid citrus
Lanterns against the teeming green,
Ready to be harvested and eaten.

— ALICIA OSTRIKER

## One More Time

And next morning, at the medical center
Though the X-Ray Room swallows me whole,

Though cold crackles in the corridors
I brace myself against it and then relax.

Lying there on the polished steel table
Though I step right out of my body,

Suspended in icy silence
I look at myself from far off
Calmly, I feel free

Even though I'm not, now
Or ever:

The metal teeth of death bite
But spit me out

One more time:

When the technician says breathe
I breathe.

— PATRICIA GOEDICKE

## At the Gynecologist's

The body so carefully
contrived for pain,
wakens from the dream of health
again and again
to hands impersonal as wax
and instruments that pry
into the closed chapters of flesh.
See me here, my naked legs
caught in these metal stirrups,
galloping towards death
with flowers of ether in my hair.

— LINDA PASTAN

## Ann: Room 8, No. 2 Biopsy with Frozen Section

Before we started, you were speaking,
Saying something to me;
Golden droplets in the tubing
Caught your eye, held your tongue;
You never finished.

When the drapes were all in place
You cried;
The tears ran sideways;
Glistening streaks upon your temples;
No one noticed.

Latex fingers, muffled voices,
Everything was bathed in blue,
It took no more than half an hour
To cut away a part of you.

— KIRK MAXEY

## A Story about the Body

The young composer, working that summer at an artist's colony,
had watched her for a week. She was Japanese, a painter, almost
sixty, and he thought he was in love with her. He loved her work,
and her work was like the way she moved her body, used her hands,
looked at him directly when she made amused and considered an-
swers to his questions. One night, walking back from a concert,
they came to her door and she turned to him and said, "I think you
would like to have me. I would like that too, but I must tell you that
I have had a double mastectomy," and when he didn't understand,
"I've lost both my breasts." The radiance that he had carried around
in his belly and his chest cavity—like music—withered, very
quickly, and he made himself look at her when he said, "I'm sorry. I
don't think I could." He walked back to his own cabin through the
pines, and in the morning he found a small blue bowl on the porch
outside his door. It looked to be full of rose petals, but he found
when he picked it up that the rose petals were on top; the rest of the
bowl—she must have swept them from the corners of her studio—
was full of dead bees.

— ROBERT HASS

## Waiting for the Doctor

I hear the doctor's loud success
booming to the anteroom,
my convent girl legs
criss-crossed at the ankles
narrowing the chapel where love huffs
like a wolf in the gray light
of redemptive sex.

Eucharistic body, tasty wafer,
Bristol-Cream sherry tapping through my veins,
Catholic outcome of a priest-father,
medieval mother on the guest bed of the parish,
witnessed by an ivory angel
and a watercolor Christ.

Waiting for the doctor, his loud success,
I think: my mother's breasts at thirty
tightening in my father's palms,
a crack inside her plaster flesh
widening for life,
my infant body's instant flush.

Disgusting girl—female scum, dirty secretions
attendant on woman's time, my mother thought
tying the parcel to mail me away.
I, reared on the assembly line,
factory for molding children into nuns.
Orphanage cookie, my cookie-self

waiting for the doctor
to come and view my masterworks:
assemblages of bone, mid-symphysial stage of decay,
sculptures for love programmed to fail,
but doubling cells under my flesh humming like a laundromat
a 9-lb. load to cart in and out of next year's bed.

— COLETTE INEZ

## Pregnancy

It is the best thing.
I should always like to be pregnant,

Tummy thickening like a yoghurt,
Unbelievable flower.

A queen is always pregnant with her country.
Sheba of questions

Or briny siren
At her difficult passage,

One is the mountain that moves
Toward the earliest gods.

Who started this?
An axis, a quake, a perimeter,

I have no decisions to master
That could change my frame

Or honor.
Immaculate. Or if it was not, perfect.

Pregnant, I'm highly explosive—
You can feel it, long before

Your seed will run back to hug you—
Squaring and cubing

Into reckless bones, bouncing odd ways
Like a football.

The heart sloshes through the microphone
Like falls in a box canyon.

The queen's only a figurehead.
Nine months pulled by nine

Planets, the moon slooping
Through its amnion sea,

Trapped, stone-mad . . . and three
Beings' lives gel in my womb.

— SANDRA MCPHERSON

# A Day in March

FOR JOAN AND MATTHEW

I awoke that day to the usual
weakness of morning: My senses
random as broken beads.
   The day before

Spring had been near:
Buds inched along paralytic twigs,
near waking, numb rumors
   that promised birth.

But that morning the buds
were gone, muffled by sudden snow
spilled over them by midnight.
   Yet birth was going on,

we knew, straining steadily
beneath those white sheets
and today we would count
   the intervals

between each spasm.
And it seemed to us
that to mark the day the world
   had slowed,

shuddered to a halt and brought
out its regal beasts, the lumbering
and lowing snowplows, to parade
   in honor of the event.

For several were trying to be born
that day: A child and a mother
and a father who would find
   their names the moment

new lungs protested the bite
of air. Snow remained,
resisting the blandishments
  of the sun;

day and night passed
and while each of you wrestled
with the problem of being born
  I sat rubbing out

cold thoughts read into my brain
by tales of broken births.
Outside, streets were clearing.
  Salt and sand

had chewed the snow to grit
and the long winter ended
when spring rode in
  on a cry.

— VERN RUTSALA

## Soft Mask

On the ultrasound screen my child curled
in his own fluid orbit, less real
than any high-school-textbook tadpole
used to symbolize birth, till the nurse
placed a white arrow on his heart flicker:
a quick needle of light. Tonight his face

blooms in my window before trees
stripped bare, a moon hung full and red.
That soft mask, not yet hardened in autumn wind,
would hold a thumbprint if I touched him. I hesitate
to touch him. He's not yet felt the burden
of a hand, nor tasted air, nor toddled
toward some bladelike gaze. He is all sweetness,
mouth smudged against the clear silk
that envelops him, webbed hands that reach
and retreat as a cat tests water.

Or like Narcissus, or the great wondering
madonnas, or any beast lost in another, the demon
who kneels to feed at some lily throat.
His pulse first matching then at odds with mine,
that small arrow seeming to tremble
as if striking something true.

— MARY KARR

## Written on Learning of Arrhythmia in the Unborn Child

I would liken woodsmoke to death
except for the birds which pass through
and emerge intact, and the sky which stands
quietly behind it, white with the chance of snow.

The horse made out of yesterday's snow
loosens its stone eyes and sculpted mane.
In time it will lose everything
except the brave forelegs, those it never had.

I could go on watching these things
until nightfall, which comes each evening
earlier now. I would sit in the inner dark
of a suburban house which burns with life,
my other children lit up from within
by ivory bones and papier-mâché complexions.
Their blood flows easy as candle wax
melted from crayon.

I could stay here in the warm pocket
that precedes shock, unlike those women
who don't feel their own faces
anymore. They walk from room to room
in the four perfect chambers
of their own hearts,

staring blankly into the future
as if it were written in chimney smoke,
carrying the past in their striated laps.
Listen as they mouth the name of the child
that was meant to be, while around them
silence widens, and the depths.

— JUDITH SKILLMAN

## The Story of the Caul

When the child woke to the world,
the caul wrapping her breath
like some cheesy cloth, her
eyes filling with the billowing

clouds, the wavering gauze—
little bride, shroud-bearer—
the doctor snipped her pale
veil at the hairline, to

sell to a sailor for luck.
She remembers, she tells me now,
the mist lifting from her face,
the milky web broken,

the opalescent lights blazing back
to her kindling brain,
the shapes swimming before her
assuming flesh, more warmth,

ever more wonder—
and she closed her blue eyes
and slept, and could have been
content not to open them again.

She knows, she tells me now,
how the world begins to come true
if we stare long enough,
if we stare hard.

*Be patient*, grandmother tells me.
*Be still, sometimes,*
*to allow the numinous net of air*
*to mend over your face.*

— MICHAEL WATERS

## To a 14 Year Old Girl in Labor and Delivery

I cannot say it to you, Mother, Child.
Nowhere now is there a trace of the guile
that brought you here. Near the end of exile

I hold you prisoner, jailer, in my cage—
with no easy remedy for your rage
against him and the child. Your coming of age

is a time of first things: a slipping of latches;
of parallels like fire and the smell of matches.
The salmon swims upstream. The egg hatches.

— JOHN STONE

## Giving Birth in Greek

Giving birth in Greek
only took two words.

The midwife smoothed my hair,
coaxed my legs into stirrups
and gave me the shot

that sent my head
high into a corner
of that dazzling room

from where I watched it all.

There was a wild animal
stuck inside me,
struggling to get out

and I could see
I was doing everything I could
to help it:

breathing evenly,
exhaling at the crest
of the contractions

not pushing

still not pushing

giving those muscles,
those raw, stubborn snails,
one last chance to break my back

and mold me into whatever shape
it needed to escape.

Then all at once
it was that moment

when I knew if I pushed
I would die

and if I didn't push
I would die
but it would still be inside me

and 'Tora!' 'Now!' she shouted

and we both bore down
and the beast became my son
and slid into her hands.

'Oraia,' 'Beautiful,'
she said. 'Oraia.'

Later, in my room, in the dark,
I started to bleed a lot
and I knew I should call the nurse

but I didn't know the words.

Anyway there were no more words.

I lay all night
in that cold, clotting stain,
wide open, wide awake

and falling in love
all over again.

— JUDITH HEMSCHEMEYER

## Childbirth

*Comment va-t-elle, Docteur?*
*Elle est parfaite, Madame.*

The distant words
swallowed by my foreign ear.

After pain,
this haze . . . this dazzle?

They say I will forget labor.

\*   \*   \*

It is February now,
and we are chilled
in the cafe until
the winter sun bursts
hotter than August
over the table.
My gloomy wine glass
quickens in the new light,
glistens, casts a shadow,
like the map in myself
filled with common boundaries.
Between my light
and my darkness . . .
those necessary neighbors.

If one of them left,
I would lose myself
in my own house.

— ANNE S. PERLMAN

## Birth

Before. there was one
Without a name

*I killed it*
*It had no heart*

One wrenched away
With a single cry

*My body floated*
*Inches above the bed*

Another drowned
In freshets of blood

*It was warm in the bed*
*But a cold hand touched my heart*

In the eyes of the newborn
I see an ancient woman

*She thinks nothing was*
*Before she came.*

— CONSTANCE URDANG

## Damage

It didn't suckle. That
was the first indication.

Looking back, I know how much I knew.
The repetitious bloodfall,

the grating at the door of bone,
the afterbirth stuck in my womb like a scab.

Others were lucky,
response was taken from them.

Each time I bathe him
in his little tub, I think

*How easy to let go*

*Let go*

— ELLEN BRYANT VOIGT

## Seizure

I gave you what I could when you were born,
salt water to rock you,
your half of nine month's meat,
miles of finished veins,
and all the blood I had to spare.

And then I said, this is the last time
I divide myself in half, the last time
I lie down in danger and rise bereft,
the last time I give up half my blood.

Fifteen months later, when I walked into your room
your mobile of the sun, moon,
and stars was tilting
while your lips twisted,
while you arched your back.

Your fingers groped for something in the air.
Your arms and legs flailed like broken wings.
Your breath was a load too heavy
for your throat to heave into your lungs.
You beat yourself into a daze against your crib.

We slapped your feet,
we flared the lights,
we doused you in a tub of lukewarm water.
But your black eyes rolled.
You had gone somewhere
and left behind a shape of bluish skin,
a counterfeit of you.
                              It was then,
before the red wail of the police car,
before the IV's, before the medicine
dropped into you like angels, before you woke
to a clear brow, to your own funny rising voice,

it was then that I would have struck the bargain,
all my blood
for your small shaking.
I would have called us even.

— JEANNE MURRAY WALKER

## The Choice

The ghost of my pregnancy, a large
amorphous vapor, much larger than me,
comes when I am alarmed to comfort me,
though it, too, alarms me, and I dodge

away, saying, "Leave me alone," and the ghost,
always beneficent, says, "You're a tough one
to do things for." The ghost must have done
this lots, it so competently knows I'm lost

and empty. It returns the fullness and slow
connection to all the world just as it is.
When I let it surround me, the embrace is
more mother than baby. How often we don't know

the difference. It's not a dead little thing
without a spinal cord yet, but a spirit of
the parent we all ought to have had, of
possibility. "I was meant to be dead." Thinking

why it said it was *meant* to be dead brings
the tangible comfort: how I used the foetus
shamelessly, how the brief pregnancy showed us,
its father and me, these choices, not shriveling

but choice alive with choice, alive with what's not
taken, or taken up, both pulsing with direction,
for some mistakes are re-takes, or correction,
past times that were forsaken now held when caught.

I never say goodbye to the ghost for
I've forgotten it's been there. That's what it's for.
The thought of the pregnancy somehow unmoors
the anxiety the choice still harbors.

— MOLLY PEACOCK

# The Watch

At this moment hundreds of women
a few miles from here are looking
for the same sign of reprieve, the red
splash of freedom. We run to check,
squirming through rituals of If I don't
look till two o'clock, if I skip lunch,
If I am good, if I am truly sorry,
probing, poking, hallucinating changes.
Flower, red lily, scarlet petunia
bloom for me. And some lesser number
of women in other bedrooms and bathrooms
see that red banner unfurl and mourn!
Another month, another chance missed.
Forty years of our lives, that flag
is shown or not and our immediate
and sometimes final fate determined,
red as tulips, red as poppies satin,
red as taillights, red as a stoplight,
red as dying, our quick bright blood.

— MARGE PIERCY

## Menstruation Rag

Played if you please
by tamponi and tuba
and accompanied by
an appropriate ritual,
say, snake, obsidian,
or the maw bone
of a buffalo, pouched
in deerskin and rattled
properly with a crisp *ye'ye'*.

But let's consider it
another way, as
theater in the round:
        "I've got dem low-down
        lunar cycle blues, daddy,"
the pitcher at the mound:
        "Two balls, one strike,
        and no outs, buster,"
one small drop for woman,
a hemorrhage for mankind.

For mankind no jam-rags,
powders, sprays, no mikvahs,
tampons, tablets, belts,
no breakthrough bleeding,
no calendar check meticulous
as a tornado watch,
no swearing on your life
in a busy cloakroom
that you're part
of the greatest show
on earth.

— DIANE ACKERMAN

## Infertility

When it gets dark
strip yourself of all garments
and lie down
on the grave of twins.
After you've said
"Springs of water, rise,
myself into myself,"
cover it with candles,
nosegays and ribbons.
You'll want to go home then.
If your husband is asleep
rub his penis with cocoanut oil
and believe
you've done everything you could.
Pass the burden, lovingly, to him.

— STEPHEN DUNN

## Mother and Child

I kiss your belly
button bursting out like
a silver dollar for your
sixth month. Sleek and
fat you sway before me,
lure me to our conjugal bed
to use each other gently before
the final lay-off.

I kiss your thighs, see
eyes staring at me from
deep inside, that wink to
say we are captured and must
pay ransom for twenty years
before we're free.

You are too sexy to be
pregnant. I am too young
to be a father. We are
too sure we need each other
to let go.

— DAVID AXELROD

## Bone Poem

The doctors, white as candles, say
*You will lose your child.*
*We will find out why.*
*We will take a photograph of your bones.*

It is the seventh month of your life.
It is the month of new lambs and foals in a field.

In the X-ray room, we crouch on an iron table.
Somebody out of sight takes our picture.

In the picture, my spine rises like cinder blocks,
my bones, scratched as an old record,
my ribs shine like the keys on a flute,
have turned to asbestos, sockets and wings.

You are flying out of the picture,
dressed in the skin of a bird.

You have folded your bones like an infant umbrella,
leaving your bone-house like a shaman.

Here we are both skeletons, pure as soap.
Listen, my little shaman, to my heart.
It is a hunter, it beats a drum all day.
    *Inside run rivers of blood, outside run rivers of water.*
    *Inside grow ships of bone, outside grow ships of steel.*

The doctor puts on his headdress.
He wears a mirror to catch your soul
which roosts quietly in my ribs.
Thank God I can tell dreaming from dying.

I feel you stretching your wings.
You are flying home.
You are flying home.

— NANCY WILLARD

## to my friend, jerina

listen,
when i found there was no safety
in my father's house
i knew there was none anywhere.
you are right about this;
how i nurtured my work
not my self, how i left the girl
wallowing in her own shame
and took on the flesh of my mother.
but listen,
the girl is rising in me,
not willing to be left to
the silent fingers in the dark.
and you are right
she is asking for more than
most men are able to give,
but she means to have what she
has earned,
sweet sighs, safe houses,
hands she can trust.

— LUCILLE CLIFTON

## Couvade

FOR H.

When your wife uttered your son
like a large syllable into this world,

you, ever the generous one, took sick too.
You took to bed and, in the large,

violent strokes that heaved beneath your belly,
it was as if you were a woman—as if by

the mere ache and purgation of your wounds
you could return to the place we have all

been exiled from; as if, by mimicking
the motions of your own child's mother,

you could be, to them and to yourself,
all things: child, father, a man so womanly

in his own being that he could, somehow,
bear his own child into the world with his wife

like a duet. It was so kind of you. And I
imagine she, too, must have known it:

How a man aches at times like these toward
places he has left and can never return to;

how he looks into the faces of his own wife
and child and staggers to bed in the sheer

empathy and pain of wanting to become them.
And how, when his wife rises from the dimmed

light of their child's afterbirth, he too
will rise, and all that is good in this world

will speak his name into the tight tercet
of their togetherness. And his son
will call him Father, and his wife: a man.

— MICHAEL BLUMENTHAL

# Rape

There is a cop who is both prowler and father:
he comes from your block, grew up with your brothers,
had certain ideals.
You hardly know him in his boots and silver badge,
on horseback, one hand touching his gun.

You hardly know him but you have to get to know him:
He has access to machinery that could kill you.
He and his stallion clop like warlords among the trash,
his ideals stand in the air, a frozen cloud
from between his unsmiling lips.

And so, when the time comes, you have to turn to him,
the maniac's sperm still greasing your thigh,
your mind whirling like crazy. You have to confess
to him, you are guilty of the crime
of having been forced.

And you see his blue eyes, the blue eyes of all the family
whom you used to know, grow narrow and glisten,
his hand types out the details
and he wants them all
but the hysteria in your voice pleases him best.

You hardly know him but now he thinks he knows you:
he has taken down your worst moment
on a machine and filed it in a file.
He knows, or thinks he knows, how much you imagined;
He knows, or thinks he knows, what you secretly wanted.

He has access to machinery that could get you put away;
and if, in the sickening light of the precinct,
and if, in the sickening light of the precinct,
your details sound like a portrait of your confessor,
will you swallow, will you deny them, will you lie your way home?

— ADRIENNE RICH

## Margo

Margo, in the grey afternoon,
sat tight. The cracked corner,
her father's chair, inhaled her frame.
She knew then she was right
to refuse the dark box
they opened
for inspection.

— FRANCINE RINGOLD

## Change of Life

Ashes of roses, forsythia bones
tulips with blackened teeth,
let me read in you
what has become of the young girl in the legend
who so craved honey
that her entire life was changed by it.

When she lay down
roses sprang from her side
her body became a trellis
for ardent tropical blooms
with corollas so deep
you could drown in them,
disappearing in those mysterious caves.

In this way the bees found her;
in the laboratory of the hive
they are transforming her into an old woman,
drained, shrivelled, and unsexual
like a quince blossom mutilated by the frost.
She has been rendered to her essences;
her voice comes to you through the lips of a crone.

— CONSTANCE URDANG

**Mental Illness:**
**The Shadow of the Obsessive Idea**

## An Invalid

My hair fans out
on pillows embroidered
with grey and green ivy.
In this dimmed room
where god has seen fit
to drop me, I make
observations, which
I note down in a small
clothbound book.
Sometimes my feet swell.
I don't mind. Amusing
little blood vessels,
delicate as the branches
of a fossil-fern
appear on my ankles.
Sometimes I get hives.
The light that ventures
in through my two windows,
is possessed of a chronic
eloquence, like the muted
light scrawled across
the floor of some
secret cathedral,
waiting to be unmasked
as random splashes
of blasphemy. My knowledge
of spiders and their ways
increases daily, although
one suspended in the corner
closest to the door seems
to have fallen from grace:
she hasn't moved for days.
I fear the worst, though one
of her relatives didn't
flinch for a week, then

produced a glob of eggs
the size of my thumbnail.
The babies emerged almost
transparent. It made me itch
to watch them scatter.

Outdoors, the ever-present
theatre of seasons provides
endless antidote to my
cultivated high-mindedness.
Glimpses of nature,
with its comforting
underlying violence
are mine to enjoy
in a truncated,
overmagnified way.
This afternoon I was
brought bread pudding
with sliced bananas,
on a tin tray
that has painted in its middle
a picture of a lake in Iceland
with an unpronounceable name.
I don't miss the dinnertime
dramas, since I still hear
the highlights from down
the hall. Last night,
my younger brother
was banished from
the dining-room almost
as soon as the main
course was served,
for putting a cigarette
out in his mashed potatoes.
Always overstepping his bounds,
he remains my favorite.

Originally bedridden
with a case of clinically
significant hiccoughs,
my ailments soon multiplied,
and became more interesting
as they accumulated.
My medicines are experimental,
highly-touted, foul-tasting—
none as hilarious or effective
as opium or ink. The canyon
behind this house is full
of flowering weeds,
and eucalyptus trees so
oily if you strike a match
in their vicinity, they'll
explode.

The outside world is terribly
crowded. All that lives
or ever came close, competes
for standing room, shouts
to be heard. Even flocks
of the stillborn, bewildered
by an unilluminating demise,
swarm around certain houses
like schools of unpoppable
bubbles. The fruity smells
of infatuation and sorrow
take up a lot of room, too,
as do unspoken complaints,
fish ponds, vegetable plots,
and all that animal magnetism
flashing between beings.
Intellectual paralysis,
that bird of prey, swoops
around, conquering scores
of minds at a time. Even

indoors, one can lose one's
foothold so easily, while
appliances hum and mind
their own business, quietly
swilling electricity. There's
no niche for me in such profusion.
I need to watch these proceedings
from the neatly shuttered windows
of my controlled environment.
I think my indefinitely prolonged
mysterious illnesses provide
the right approach. To lull
myself to sleep at night,
I close my eyes and begin
by visualizing what's overhead,
and then working my way down.
*Planets, stars, clouds,*
*mountain summits, radio towers*
*atop skyscrapers, crowns*
*of the tallest trees, our weathervane,*
*our roof* (which needs re-shingling),
*my ceiling, my tile floor, the house's*
*cement slab foundation, the crust*
*of the dirt, animal burrows*
*in the first crumbly layers of soil,*
*and deeper down,* (because the best
is always saved for last) *worms*
*turning like white screws*
*in the chocolatey earth.*

— AMY GERSTLER

## Landscape

The dimensions are dizzying; peaks
unraveling the sky, light sheer

as rock unbroken by leaves or shrubs
or the humble shadows of passersby.

In this wilderness, I must invent
my own markers, a way of describing

distances only my body knows.
I'm like the first settlers who tried to stake out

a plot in rampant space: nights,
the frail structure of belief crumbles.

And yet you look at me and see a woman
like any other; you don't see

the landscape of illness, the cliffs
within myself I scale each day.

— MARGUERITE BOUVARD

## The Legacy

No need to dial the doctor. I have
already heard that it flows in the genes,
floats on invisible electric currents
perhaps, from mother to son
to daughter, the mother again.

I have been to that old barn, looked
up through the dusting sunlight
from loft to splintered rafter; have almost
seen the rope, the empty space full with her
sagging skirt and dangling legs.

I have listened, but they never speak
her name, that grandmother
shrouded in dust, the grave
marked with whispers that sin begets sinner.
I have ceased to pray to the Virgin.

No matter. Yesterday I saw fire
in a cat's eye, touched the coarse mane
of a wild horse, at last set my house
in order. At night
clouds form in front of the moon.

— JUDITH MINTY

## Rorschach Test

I am to hold the pictures as I wish,
Look as long as I wish, and tell you all
I see—wholes, parts, details, or anything.
There are no wrong answers. Anything goes.
Yet you will not say what my answers tell you,
And I am being tested knowing so.
I launch a boomerang at a shadowy mark
Of indefinite size at an unknown distance.

   I see a bat with islands and a bear,                         I
But mostly pelvis. Then bears join snouts in a V;      II
Though they are gentle teddy bears, their feet
Stand in blood, and a blood-cloud floats above.
(Viewed upside down, there are bloody little puppets;
Satan leers; there is a cave in the middle.)
Twin footmen bow over a roasted crab,                  III
With hovering blood in the sky. (Seen from above,
Always the pelvis, sutured with a zipper.)
   Then looms King Darkness, zip-sex at the bottom.     IV
A pelt laid out on a slab, and little lizards.
Another zippered bat, clam-valves, proboscis.            V
A dead goose with a few neck-feathers clinging.        VI
Its soft raccoon-fur zippered all the way;
Clouds, with an elephant, pelvis at the top,            VII
With faces. Bison-foxes going down,                VIII
With blue, green, pink, and lurid; liver ice-cream
Dripping down from the top. (I do not see
The lampshade—not very commonly observed—
Perhaps only by the gifted or disturbed.
Nor do I note the Grand Lama, seen
By one in a million—idiot or Einstein?)
   The stimuli are being switched on me;           IX
Things are no longer quite symmetrical:
An arc-halo over green, orange, and rose;
Tree-witches with fingers; the face of Mark Twain;
Blood boils up through a tube (perhaps Fallopian).

Then drunken fireworks in all colors, loud
As the last salvo on the Fourth of July;
Yellow elephant-butterflies and a blue crab,
Pink shad-roe at the side; green caterpillars
Join heads or tails to make a fertile rabbit;
And sepia monsters out of Jerome Bosch
Converse in eighteenth-century rhymed couplets,
Erecting in the sky a pole-and-hole.
    Take them away. I have told you enough.
They are like rain-stains on my childhood ceiling,
Unchanging, but never twice suggesting
The same shadows, and always ominous.
I am to go over them a second time?—
Pointing out where I saw things and then listing
Others I have forgotten—or repressed?
You have found out too much about me already.
One horned beast more, one zippered pelvis less,
Would smoke me out of sepia into sunlight.
Though you do not say so, where there are no wrong
Answers, there can be no right answers.
    I must see enough and not too much, must talk
Enough and not too much, must say I see
What the well-adjusted person says he sees.
I want to be like everybody else
But not too much like everybody else.
Though I may have failed this test you set for me,
I am not compelled to go through it again.

— SPENCER BROWN

## Agoraphobia

It isn't that she doesn't
want to go to the marketplace, if only
to buy one small
compliment. She can remember each
time she went,
got one, took it
home, put it in
a porcelain cup she kept
beside her bed.
She stopped
going out for fear

of wanting too much to fill
the fragile container,
decorated her house in muted
stripes
and moved onto her bed
a color TV

which she watches
steadily.
She likes the news, especially
the accidents that happen
when people travel too far
from home.
They secure her place.
And when she faces
a scene filled with a good
time, she wanders—
but only in her mind.

— SUSAN HAHN

## The Improvement

These are the addicts of charts,
the anxious who wait for crises
and side effects, their eyes geared
to read only the scrawls of doctors.
They sit in their lawn chairs
at late evening, hoping the voices
from the high grass will stop,
that they will someday hold
a mower in their hands again
and never sit undressed while doctors
thump their chests like melons.
Something will happen, they know.
The latest abscess applying for admission
to their flesh will prove a fraud;
their x-rays will turn out to be
those of someone else; and they
will be made to lose their appetite
for the fumes of motors in locked garages.
But the voices go on, calling them
to join the dark burrowers, the faint
turners of soil, on vacant lots
where only the dismembered
or decaying are discovered.
But they always save their shining
trump for late evening's final
desolation: They say all weakness
finds its compensation—the blind
hear the steps of ants, the deaf read
whispers and the incurable never die.

— VERN RUTSALA

# In Such an Unhappy Neighborhood, Carlos

BEN TAUB HOSPITAL, 3-S, PSYCHIATRY

The nylon crescent of her pink panties hangs in the sky
And I can't slip on anything or into
Something comfortable because Mama always told me
"You're the man now, now he's gone. Be a good boy,"
But I wouldn't turn down a green silk robe or a bed
Because Mama, listen to me, you know I do wear the pants.

The others were jealous because I was born under
A special moon with the great scorpion rising
And ram horns battering the smeary streak
Of milk in black sky like a needle in
A Carmen Dios record and today I wore grey ones over khakis
Over my jeans because it is cold for July.

And they were jealous because I went to school
And got a round, gold medal and because I knew so much
That they sliced the watermelon into halves like a moon
With that green rim giving warning and they seeded
The dark pink flesh with something because they were jealous
And they wanted me stupid the way they were.

And I bit into the flesh of the melon moon
And Perdita danced for me in her shiny yellow skirt
And I knew I was slipping down Truxillo Street
As if it were a banana peel and broke every bone in my body.
But they didn't get me stupid. All I can see
Is the nylon crescent of her pink panties hanging
On the post of my bed and I keep asking—can't you hear—
When can I see my Mama?

— CYNTHIA MACDONALD

## To Make a Dragon Move:
## From the Diary of an Anorexic

*It would have starved a gnat*
*To live so small as I —*
*And yet I was a living Child —*
*With food's necessity*

*Upon me like a Claw*
*I could no more remove*
*Than I could coax a leech away —*
*Or make a Dragon — move —*

—EMILY DICKINSON, NO. 612

I have rules and plenty. Some things I don't touch.
I'm king of my body now. Who needs a mother—
a food machine, those miles and miles of guts?
Once upon a time, I confess, I was fat—
gross. Gross belly, gross ass, no bones
showing at all. Now I say, "No, thank you," a person
in my own right, and no poor loser. I smile
at her plate of brownies. "Make it disappear,"

she used to say, "Join the clean plate club." I disappear
into my room where I have forbidden her to touch
anything. I was a first grade princess once. I smile
to think how those chubby pinks used to please my mother.
And now that I am, Dear Diary, a sort of magical person,
she can't see. My rules. Even here I don't pour out my guts.
Rules. The writing's slow, but like picking a bone,
satisfying, and it doesn't make you fat.

Like, I mean, what would I want with a fat
Diary! Ha ha. But I don't want you to disappear
either. It's tricky . . . "Form in a poem is like the bones
in a body," my teacher says. (I wish he wouldn't touch

me—ugh!—he has B.O.—and if I had the guts
I'd send him a memo about it, and about his smile.
Sucking the chalk like he does, he's like a person
with leprosy.) I'm too sensitive, so says Mother.

She thinks Mr. Crapsie's Valentino. If my so-called mother
is getting it on with him behind my back, that fat
cow . . . What would he see in her? Maybe he likes a person
to have boobs like shivery jello. Does he want to disappear
between thighs like tapioca? His chalky smile
would put a frosting on her Iced Raspberry, his "bone"
(another word for IT, Sue said) would stick in her gut,
maybe, bitten right off! Now why did I have to touch

on that gross theme again, when I meant to touch
on "thoughts too deep for tears," and not my mother.
That Immortality thing, now—I just have a gut
reaction to poems like that—no "verbal fat"
in poems like that, or in "the foul rag and bone
shop of the heart." My God! How does a person
learn to write like that? Like they just open to smile
and heavy words come out. Like, I just *disappear*

beside that stuff. I guess that's what I want: to disappear.
That's pretty much what the doctor said, touching
me with his icy stethoscope, prying apart my smile
with that dry popsicle stick, and he said it to Mother.
And now all she says is "What kind of crazy person
would starve herself to death?" There I am, my gut
flipflopping at the smell of hot bread, my bone
marrow turning to hot mud as she eases the fat

glistening duck out of the microwave, the fat
swimming with sweet orange. I wish it would disappear,
that I . . . If I could just let myself suck a bone—
do bones have calories?—I wouldn't need to touch
a bite of anything else. I am so empty. My gut

must be loopy thin as spaghetti. I start to chew my smile.
Is lip-skin fattening? I know Hunger as a person
inside me, half toad, half dwarf. I try to mother

him: I rock and rock and rock him to sleep like a mother
by doing sit-ups. He leans his gargoyle head against the fat
pillow of my heart. But awake he raves, a crazy person,
turned on by my perpetual motion, by the disappearing
tricks of my body; his shaken fist tickles drool to my smile.
He nibbles at my vagus nerve for attention. Behind the bone
cage of my chest, he is bad enough. He's worse in my gut
where his stamped foot means binge and puke. Don't touch

me, Hunger, Mother . . . Don't you gut my brain.
Bones are my sovereign now, I can touch them here and here.
I am a pure person, magic, revealed as I disappear
into my final fat-free smile, where there is no pain.

— PAMELA WHITE HADAS

## The Shulamite Girl

> *Return, return, O Shulamite, return*
> *that we may look upon thee.*
> —SOLOMON'S SONG

The doctor with Lake Tahoe in his eyes
has charts of an outlined, white-space man
whose colored meridians strike
his insides like the arrows of St. Sebastian.
The large, cement-gray-suited woman
who has driven with her son
from Sacramento sits before the doctor
and says she's the wife of Solomon.
"I am the Shulamite Girl," she says.
"And not only that," lifting her voice
like a tin cup, "I know for a fact
I am the bride of Christ."

The doctor shifts his clipboard
to the other knee. His pale assistant
shoots some liquid into other liquid
with a hypodermic, trying not to listen.
"Twenty-four years ago,"
the Shulamite Girl goes on,
"they locked me in a little cell.
No one came except my son.
When I got out after a year
with those crazy people, I told them
I was still the Shulamite Girl
and they locked me up again."

The doctor has a mind like the wood floor.
Her voice makes sharp, irritating sounds
upon it. After a few more
sentences he focuses behind her:
the hundred little cloudy amber vials

surrounding them like well-wishers,
the rolltop desk heaped with disheveled files
of other schizophrenics;
he watches a private plane scrape
the green hills like a razor,
his eyes wander to the charts, the mauve drapes—
there is no remedy for the Shulamite Girl.

You hover at the brink of nonexistence
with your soul-destroying love,
recalling the trees of frankincense,
the poetry of spices: saffron, myrrh, and cinnamon;
and after you've cross-referenced everything—
mandrakes and the names of cities—
you're still in the service of some abstract king
and you say of yourself, I am a wall,
knowing that even wrong dreams
might bear some benefits; as he has two
armies, you have the aquamarine
canopy of your belief.

— BRENDA HILLMAN

## Wait

Six beds in a square room; you give your name
And sleep for days. Then the comeback—the shame,
The Thorazine, and long walks in the sun
As thought retreats from the oblivion
It took on trust. And through it all, you sense
Only your ruin and fatigue as dense
As sleep. What happened? They won't answer you,
But just solicit your submission to
The judgement they'll "in due time" formulate.
And till then? Get some rest. Be patient. Wait.

— TIMOTHY STEELE

## The Suicide

I drink this whiskey from a window overlooking the sea,
The fierce plunge
Fixed at the back of my skull.
Bicycles roar like breakers down the shore.
In twos and threes the riders disappear,
Taking my life in their wheels.
Gulls scream as I dive.
Oh, fish, have I hated enough?
Let's sleep in silence. This is no dream.
The birds have murdered the trees.

— DAVID POSNER

## Suicide's Note

The calm,
Cool face of the river
Asked me for a kiss.

— LANGSTON HUGHES

## To a Young Woman Considering Suicide

When everything you touch is already touched,
you can't sleep, can't eat, can't even
remember when you could, you go on living;

When everywhere you are you want to leave,
it's so stupid, stupid not to go down
with the sun, down with leaves spiralling,

Down with the duck pulled under
by the muskrat, waves, they don't roll in,
they roll down and die—even now, you go on living.

Would you help me with my plant?
See, it's not doing well at all, and out
there in the snow my friend's car is stuck.

He needs a hand. What do you think?—
More light? A bigger pot? And what do I say
to my child, to your child perhaps someday,
if she goes out, as you have, under the long shadow?

— PETER SEARS

## In the Place Where the Corridors
## Watch Your Every Move

In the place where the corridors watch your every move,
In the place of the gossiping psychiatrists who pass
What their patients say around like children playing
Telephone, until the message that said Help me has become
The sky has disappeared, leaving nothing in its place,

In the place where bewigged judges disguise themselves as bearded
    psychiatrists,
In the place of rooms that do not lock and of rooms that lock
Only from the outside, in the place of misery beyond telling, in the
    place of weeping
And white fluted flowers that bloom in trays at regular hours, a
    pink or blue
Or golden seed splitting at its heart while the corridors watch
    your every move,

In the place of the talking doctors whose definitions are all
    synonyms
And the place of the patients who have nothing to say, since what
    the patients say,
The doctors translate, thinking, because they have been given
    degrees and because
Their dictionaries may be modified by majority vote at the APA,
    that they understand
The language, in the place where the corridors watch your every
    move,

Someone was saying Help me help me I am frightened
Because the sky has disappeared, leaving nothing in its place.

— KELLY CHERRY

## To D——, Dead by Her Own Hand

My dear, I wonder if before the end
You ever thought about a children's game—
I'm sure you must have played it too—in which
You ran along a narrow garden wall
Pretending it to be a mountain ledge
So steep a snowy darkness fell away
On either side to deeps invisible;
And when you felt your balance being lost
You jumped because you feared to fall, and thought
For only an instant: that was when I died.

That was a life ago. And now you've gone,
Who would no longer play the grown-ups' game
Where, balanced on the ledge above the dark,
You go on running and don't look down,
Nor ever jump because you fear to fall.

— HOWARD NEMEROV

## Dropping toward Stillness

Her mind is a stone    dull
and smooth at the edges

Even the voices she loves
sound strange    and muffled
passing through phones
and long-distance handkerchiefs

There are people who say
they know her    attendants
who fix the wires    and believe
that shock is therapeutic
that the first principle
is to keep moving    to stay
awake    not to go mute

Inside it gets quieter
and the secret box she lives in
makes motion harder

She means to tell them that
but the words latch in
Her throat is shutting down.

— ROSE MARCEL

## Claustrophobia

The feeling started in the womb,
there wasn't room enough
for her.
Voices from the other side
spoke of how they hoped
it was a boy.
She wanted to run,
unravel from the fetal knot,

but couldn't
ease into the narrow
passageway, persuade herself
it was an opening.
So they cut her out
a wider door
and she began careful
not to get too close.
Now, when she's forced

into a crowded place
she always imagines
being stuck in
other people's displeasures.
She returns to a crawlway
full of old alarm
and is caught
angry and unborn.

— SUSAN HAHN

## Schizophrenic Girl

Having crept out this far,
So close your breath casts moisture on the pane,
Your eyes blank lenses opening part way
To the dead moonmoth fixed with pins of rain,
Why do you hover here,
A swimmer not quite surfaced, inches down,
Fluttering water, making up her mind
To breathe, or drown?

All the fall long, earth deepening its slant
Back from the level sun, you wouldn't quit
That straitbacked chair they'd dress you in. You'd sit,
Petrified fire, casting your frozen glare,
Not swallowing, refusing to concede
There are such things as spoons. And so they'd feed
You through a vein
Cracked open like a lake they'd icefish in—
Can no one goad
You forth into the unsteady hearthlight of the sane?

Already, yawning child
At some dull drawn-out adult affair,
You whimper for permission to retire
To your right room where black
T-squares of shadows lie, vacuity
A sheet drawn halfway back.

If you'd just cry. Involved
Around some fixed point we can't see, you whirl
In a perpetual free-fall.
Come forth. We cannot stand
To see turned into stone what had been hand,
What had been mind smoothed to a bright steel ball.

— X. J. KENNEDY

## Evening in the Sanitarium

The free evening fades, outside the windows fastened with
    decorative iron grilles.
The lamps are lighted; the shades drawn; the nurses are watching a
    little.
It is the hour of the complicated knitting on the safe bone needles;
    of the games of anagrams and bridge;
The deadly game of chess; the book held up like a mask.

The period of the wildest weeping, the fiercest delusion, is over.
The women rest their tired half-healed hearts; they are almost well.
Some of them will stay almost well always: the blunt-faced woman
    whose thinking dissolved
Under academic discipline; the manic-depressive girl
Now leveling off; one paranoiac afflicted with jealousy.
Another with persecution. Some alleviation has been possible.

O fortunate bride, who never again will become elated after
    childbirth!
O lucky older wife, who has been cured of feeling unwanted!
To the suburban railway station you will return, return,
To meet forever Jim home on the 5:35.
You will be again as normal and selfish and heartless as anybody
    else.

There is life left: the piano says it with its octave smile.
The soft carpets pad the thump and splinter of the suicide to be.
Everything will be splendid: the grandmother will not drink
    habitually.
The fruit salad will bloom on the plate like a bouquet
And the garden produce the blue-ribbon aquilegia.
The cats will be glad; the fathers feel justified; the mothers relieved.
The sons and husbands will no longer need to pay the bills.
Childhoods will be put away, the obscene nightmare abated.

At the ends of the corridors the baths are running.
Mrs. C. again feels the shadow of the obsessive idea.
Miss R. looks at the mantel-piece, which must mean something.

— LOUISE BOGAN

## Counting the Mad

This one was put in a jacket,
This one was sent home,
This one was given bread and meat
But would eat none,
And this one cried No No No No
All day long.

This one looked at the window
As though it were a wall,
This one saw things that were not there,
This one things that were,
And this one cried No No No No
All day long.

This one thought himself a bird,
This one a dog,
And this one thought himself a man,
An ordinary man,
And cried and cried No No No No
All day long.

— DONALD JUSTICE

## Shocking Treatment

It's been four years now since my first attempt—
the one it took me years to own as such,
the one I made in terror, crazed for want
of sleep, on the spur of a moment in
my parents' house. Four years. The statute's time
is more than up. Though I never have been
the litigious type, my conscience exceeds
limitations; speak it must. Think back now:
I was ill; your practice of medicine
nearly killed me, plucked two years from my life.

Your first mistake was to see me at all.
Your second, prescribing the Elavil.
Your third—unseemly, unconscionable—
disregarding the symptoms I divulged:
sleeplessness, electricity streaming
through my arms and legs. Ever my mother's
psychiatrist, you dismissed these both as
*minor side effects.* To my father you
confess, in retrospect, you'd never dreamt
I might be a *bipolar,* offer to
do a credentials check on whoever
succeeds my shrink. By word and deed you try
my patience, compel me to explore how
much standard error I can grin and bear.

Not long ago, for a friend I surveyed
the PDR on Elavil. Reading
PRECAUTIONS gave me quite a shock: *Depressed
patients with manic-depressive illness
may shift to mania.* Old news, but how
those printed words sizzled in basic black
on white! Their message surged from eyes to mind
to heart: A competent psychiatrist
would have that text by heart. I'm no M.D.,

just a bipolar, returned from the dread
antipodes to advise.
                    ***Physician,***
practitioner of the healing art; swear
this oath: *No doctor is divine.* Human
frailty, no higher authority, defines
everyone. One shattered survivor stands
before you, exalts life's pieces, pardons
herself, goes on, reciting the doctrine
it seems you have neglected all along:
***Heal*** *thyself!* Soul-searching begins at home.

— RIKA LESSER

## From a Girl in a Mental Institution

The morning wakes me as a broken door vibrating on its
hinges.
We are drifting out to sea this morning. I
can barely feel the motion of the boat as it rocks me.
I must be a gull, sitting on the mast,
else why would I be so high above the world?
Yes.
I see everything down there—
children tucked, sleeping, into the waves,
their heads nestled in foam
        *AND I DON'T LIKE THE WAVES THEY*
        *DISTINCTLY SAY THINGS*
        *AGAINST ME.*
The wind is blowing my feathers. How good
that feels. If the wind
had always blown my feathers, I would
never have cried
when the waves spoke
that way—
taking my brother away, when he dove in and never came
back.
        it was because he loved the seashells
        too much
        i know
        and broken water foams in my hair
        in its new color—the color of my wing
Why don't we hear the fog-horns today?
        *IF I AM TO SIT HERE ALL DAY I MUST*
        *HAVE SOMETHING TO LISTEN TO.*
The waves have torn the sleeping children to bits. I
see them scattered on the crests now.
There—an arm floating by.
        leave me alone, i have not hurt you
        Stop pulling my wings,
        my beak, *DON'T YOU HEAR STOP IT.*

There is nothing more horrible than hands
like ancient crabs, pulling at one. And they cannot
hear because they have no ears.
      I have no ears.
I am a gull. Birds have no ears. I cannot hear
Them
or anyone.
The fingers on the dismembered arm, floating
in the waves,
can point and make signs,
but I will not hear
the waves
telling the fingers odious things about me.
I will not watch their obscenities
pointing to the bottom where the children are buried;
where he is buried;
where I am buried.

Slam the door as often as you like—you will
not wake me.
I am a gull
sitting on the mast, and I feel the ocean rocking
because I can hear nothing
but silent voices the wind carries from the past—
      gently rocking.
The ocean is as still as a newly made bed,
rocking.

 — D I A N E  W A K O S K I

## The Invisible Woman

The invisible woman in the asylum corridor
sees others quite clearly,
including the doctor who patiently tells her
she isn't invisible,
and pities the doctor, who must be mad
to stand there in the asylum corridor,
talking and gesturing
to nothing at all.

The invisible woman has great compassion.
So, after a while, she pulls on her body
like a rumpled glove, and switches on her voice
to comfort the elated doctor with words.
Better to suffer this prominence
than for the poor young doctor to learn
he himself is insane.
Only the strong can know that.

— ROBIN MORGAN

## At the Hospital

On the garden bench of the hospital,
Resting behind trim hedges in the shade,
My friend looks peaceful for the first time.
"Good thoughts," he explains, "make a good life.
So I sit here all day thinking good thoughts:
How many more little threads
Reach out by evening from this bench
To tie themselves to fences and barns.
The faintest twitching of my hand,
The ghost of a wish to haul them in,
Would break each one. So I sit still,
My fingers like stone, my bench
The quiet tether of the world.

"Do you see those patients over there,
How they wedge their faces between the fence bars
To stare at the road? These are the ones
Who wake me at night with crying.
Should I make myself join in out of fellowship,
Pretending to cry so they won't feel alone?
That would be a thread from my bench to theirs.
But they, reaching out, needy and ignorant,
Would break what might have held for years."

— CARL DENNIS

## Visit to My Committed Grandma

Though she is small and clean and neat,
Standing before me, whom I greet
I fear, as if the old could see
Something terrible in me
And cry it out. Her dress, her skin
(No starch can smooth) conceals within
What will not let us recognize
Our kinship, though her chewing eyes
Come close; I have another name,
Am "dear," and "fool," have loved, caused shame,
Until she, begging, cries to me
For failure of identity . . .
His, or hers, or mine? I come
To pity, but am finally dumb
Before this ancient being where time
Is nothing, fear, or its sublime
Of love is lastly all. The nurse
Insists today is somehow worse
And brings her milky glass of drugs
For what beneath those wrung-out dugs
Went wild, headlong, back and deep,
And needs, returning, childlike sleep
And not my pity; yet I claim
More kinship than a dubious name,
To show her (if I could) the mark,
This family wears, most bright in dark,
And, stranger though I seem, I bear:
The self like one bad dream we share.

— LEONARD NATHAN

## The Asylum

I

I came to this place one November day.
Mauve walls rose up then tranquilly, and still
Must rise to wind-burned eyes that way—
Old brickwork on a hill,
Surfaces of impunity beneath a gray
And listed sky. Yet I could read dismay
There rightward in a twisted beech
Whose nineteen leaves were glittering, each
A tear in a rigid eye caught in the pale
Deep-pouring wind. Now these walls
Are thin against the dense insistent gale,
No good when the wind talks in our halls,
Useless at night when these high window bars
Catch every whisper of wind that comes and falls,
Speaking, across my catacomb of stars.

— HAYDEN CARRUTH

**Disability:**
**Their Lockstep Tight as Lilac Buds**

## The Affect of Elms

Across the narrow street from the old hotel that now
houses human damage temporarily—
deranged, debilitated, but up and around in their odd
postures, taking their meds, or maybe trading them—

is the little park, once a neighboring mansion's side yard,
where beautiful huge old elm trees, long in that place,
stand in a close group over the mown green lawn
watered and well kept by the city, their shapes expressive:

the affect of elms is of struggle upward and survival,
of strength—despite past grief (the bowed languorous arches)
and torment (limbs in the last stopped attitude of writhing)—

while under them wander the deformed and tentative
persons, accompanied by voices, counting their footsteps,
exhaling the very breath the trees breathe in.

— REGINALD GIBBONS

## Day Ten after Heart Surgery, Signing a Check

Bending forward on ratchets
as if she might again break
open breastbone to navel
or spring the ribcage
they had to saw through
to make good the heart inside

my mother signs on the correct line
an alien name—
like hers, but with consonants doubled
m's and n's drunk on their rises
like a needle stuck
loving one note

and I don't want to hear it
but I'm afraid of picking the arm up,
scratching the record.
I point, fetch her other glasses
and still the letters convene
too fast for her to grasp.

Seventy years ago
in the one-room schoolhouse
she learned words,
carried her name over snowdrifts,
gave it shining back
to her mother and father, earth-turners.

Now she must sign again
I say, banks are skeptics.
My breath climbs each extra curve
while we try to stay calm.
For this teaching, nothing
prepares me, nor for her
I'm so stupid

until here surfaces Miss Covell
who drilled me in penmanship.
Slow, I say. Go slow, and count each hill

as alive, beside me, needing cash
my mother signs her name.

— CAROLE SIMMONS OLES

## Another Tree

*If a tree dies, plant another one.* —LINNAEUS

We sat in the yard where his house had burned.

Only I had seen the shadowed negative,
the x-ray of his brain. He squinted,

one eye too sensitive to the sun.

His right hand lay useless on his lap.
Optimism all that was left to him,

all of his grace.

For him, I'd rescued and rebuilt the place,
made a new house, planted another tree,

the little mimosa now two stories high.

In a few weeks, he'd be gone,
such was the rapaciousness of the cells,

so defenseless the nervous system.

This was the yard, this the driveway,
where one summer of Saturdays, he gathered

*minyans* to say *Kaddish* for his mother.

He admired every thing living, he loved
the mimosa, the pan-sized hibiscus,

the woodpecker whose staccato knocks
are the punctuation of this memory.

I held his good left hand, still the dreamer,

*"Look what a miracle this hand is —"*
he said, *"seventy years I hardly used it,*

*and now, the things it's learning to do!"*
We looked together at what was left,

at what was growing.

— GAIL MAZUR

## A Memory

My father's corn is knee-high for the Fourth
and his left side is stronger,
but he hasn't whipped
the grass into shape
and he broods
about a brassy hen pheasant
that flutters into his dreams
to nest on his heart.
He likes her,
he likes her better than all those
damn pills the doctor makes him buy!
Twice one night she got him up
but that's all right—
he ate cereal in the moonlight,
and walked in the long grass, drifting back
to his father's farm.
There was new snow on the ground
and Brownie, the collie, lay covered with it.
Barefoot
he went out
and reached under
to feel her, to make sure she was breathing,
and to say, Come to bed,
I have a nice fat hen
who will keep us warm.

— GARY GILDNER

## Stroke Patient

Someone came in to ask
how are you

only I couldn't
quite hear the words,
I thought he was asking
who. who are you?

so I started to say
my name's Jordan
only I never
got past the vowel

I'm Joe
just Joe
call me Joe

then I stopped to think
maybe I really am
someone else
maybe all this never
happened

my friend looked so strange to me
till I felt his hand—
his hand took mine
and my hand shook.

— ROCHELLE RATNER

# The Handicapped

**1**

The missing legs
Of the amputee
Are away somewhere
Winning a secret race.

**2**

The blind man has always stood
Before an enormous blackboard,
Waiting for the first
Scrawl of light,
That fine
Dusty chalk.

**3**

Here
The repetitions of the stutterer,
There
The flickering of the stars.

**4**

Master of illusion,
The paralytic alone moves.
All else is still.

**5**

At Creation,
God told the deaf,
"Only you will hear
The song of the stone."

**6**

Dare not ask
What the dumb
Have been told to keep secret.

**7**

When the epileptic
Falls in a fit,
He is ascending
To the heaven of earth.

— PHILIP DACEY

## Rehabilitation Center

In the good suburb, in the bursting season,
their canes awag in the yellow day,
the newly maimed mince back to danger.

Cave by cave they come to build their hearing
hard as fists against the jangling birds,
the slipslop of car wheels, walls' mimicries,

the hollow rebuttal of planes. Curbs curse them.
Puddles damn their simplicity. At lot lines
forsythia is a swipe across the face.

Under a wide sky let them cry now
to be coddled, misread a tree, black shins,
or crack their knees on countermands;

the downgrade is uncertain for us all.

In time they will grow competent,
love us, test and correct, feel words
on their quiet skin, begin to light our lamps.

Six weeks and they will swing around these corners,
grotesque and right, their appetites restored.
It is true the sun is only heat,

but distance, depth, doorsills
are ridged on their maps until
they know exactly where they are now.

I see their lockstep tight as lilac buds.

— MAXINE KUMIN

## The Game

You are my friends. You do things
for me. My affliction is
your hangup. It is yours more
than it ever could be mine.
You spread my affliction thin

enough to go around once
for all of us. You put my
coat on for me when I ask
you. You put my coat on for
me when I do not ask you.

You embrace my shoes with your
compassion. You tell me I
would be less apt to fall with
rubber soles. You carry things
for me. You tell me they are

heavy things, how it would be
difficult for anyone
to carry them. You open
mustard bottles for me. You
tell me how hard it is to

open mustard bottles. I
agree with you. I will not
destroy our game. At night I
dream I am Samson. I will
topple coliseums. I

will overwhelm you with my
brute power. I will knock you
dead. I will open mustard

bottles for you. I will show
you how easy it really is.

— HAROLD BOND

## Global Aphasia

It's like a two-way street, the hospital speech
therapist explains, drawing lanes with arrows

and curves. Information swerves in through the ears;
replies arrive in the mouth. The brain is the driver.

"Okay okay okay," Mother answers without delay
when asked about the food, her health, this task.

This "automatic response," a kind of static, relieves
the silence she emotes like a high-frequency note

of distress. "Brush your . . . ?" "Suitcase," she rushes to fill
in the blank, shaking her head as you would to free the ink

in a ballpoint pen. "Tie your . . . ?" Mother's eyes roll.
"Suitcase?" she pleads. At the root of "perseveration," the name

for this odd repeating of words, is the word "persevere,"
that hopeful bird which sits on my chest with its head

snaked under a wing and its talons digging in as she shakes
more and more suitcases loose from her mind. One shines

on her finger, one barks like a dog. O singer with your one-word
song, you knew I was there but not for how long, so all day

you conjured up luggage, all afternoon you lured my bags
from the thicket of thought and picked at the locks of my visit.

— ENID SHOMER

## Enid Field: In Memoriam

An agile voice, quick smile, and leaping eyes:
among the verities that bore her name,
and these things made one slow to realize,
quite incidentally, that she was lame.

The way she laughed if someone pitied her!
Calamity was just a kind of cloak
that one should wear akimbo, as it were,
with easy nonchalance—a kind of joke
was tragedy, that postured like a clown:
a trouble gone theatrical with age,
a grief got up in greasepaint, whose renown
depended on trick lighting and a stage.

Upheld by brace and crutch to common sight,
her grace was consummate, her footstep light.

— GLORIA MAXSON

## A Question of Energy

I'm not diminished
   by this loss of limb
I'm more than
   the sum of my parts
to deny my scars
   is to deny my power
the core of heat in each cell.

I've got wires humming
   juice surging
     detours on the path
it takes less time now
less resistance
to complete the circuit

   I'm well grounded
     you can touch me
       without a shock.

— AMBER COVERDALE SUMRALL

## The Stroke

attacks while he's on the toilet,
thin dull pain and yellow stars.
The bright world dies.

His new self wakes contracted
dry.
He starts again
can't finish.

His numbness struggles
with oatmeal, loses to
his once fastidious chin.
Words are boulders
that roll on his tongue,
burst.

Gray shadows of family
gather
in too loud blurred TV.
Decisions
hang in the closet,
time rusts shut.

He dozes with half a world
in each eye
waits with animal cries
on the collar of hope.

His blazing pride
his fractured will
his vanity
can't thaw his frozen wrist.

— CHRISTOPHER FAHY

## Angles

Gram died with most of her joints frozen
  At right angles. My childhood watched
   Her form brittle until she couldn't walk;
    After that her frame assumed unchosen

    Angles of the wheelchair and cracked like deadwood.
   When I see my father now, I feel
    A bloodrush back: his spine congeals
    From the hips a rigid angle forward.

     As in some half-forgotten dream
     I've lived a future; it persists
     In hard lumps on my wrists,
      A bamboo gait and a grip growing lame.

      Here where I live the trees grow at a slant
      To northeast with the wind; they calcify
      In traction. Across from my early
       Years, trees grow straight along the ditchbank,

      Each shaped like an ostrich feather.
      Enchanted child, I think they've volatile
      Powers to create the wind as they will
      By fanning still air.

— DIXIE PARTRIDGE

## The Tingle

My body fell asleep years ago. Cut off
at my neck by shattered bone fragments,
the line of my spine was bizarre. Alert,
my mind and soul prayed over my body's comas
for the burial of the dead, for the body's
resurrection. Spasms were electro-therapy
that increased its voltage as my muscles
twitched in an embryonic retreat to gain
again the lost dance of running grass anew.
Fire. My bed on fire! Quick, get a nurse!
"Is my bed on fire? Don, is my bed on fire?"
My skin was blazing. I tossed myself just
inches about with spasms, with arms a-fire,
flaying at imagined fires burning beneath me
burning through the mattress and rubber sheet,
burning the returning nerves into finite
disaster and no hope of repair. Time. Hurry.
Doctor help me. Doctor see me. Doctor. Doctor.
They came in answer to my pounding heart,
with white faces of care as we all feared
destruction beyond control. The sheets were
flung. The mattress shoved and bent. Ten arms
help me above the floor away from the fire.
I was saved. I felt saved. I felt love. All
of the faces of my friends began to smile.
Saved. We all loved our saving gift. All
having done all that there was to do. Fire?
Not a spark. Not a singe. No smoke. My spine
was a flaming tree within me with the flames
reaching my flesh, as I healed into wakefulness.
My body awakening in a flash from hell and
I lay burning in bed. All touch was flame but
I was a mystic lying on hot coals, not fearing
fires that eased into a tingle, the awakening
of sleeping hands. Today the slight tingle

of my body is a sensation few will know.
Unlike electric sparks, my skin does not dazzle
from the fire within and hands, all kinds of hands,
are like warm water, a kiss that takes fire's hot
melting into the warm glow of a natural comfort
as snug as body love, relaxed without release,
without the climactic claim of final conquest.
Hold me, if only in illusion. Feel the kicking stop.

— NORMAN ANDREW KIRK

## The Old Hoofer

If my legs cannot move
I will wriggle my toes
Till they learn
To do intricate dances.

— LILLIAN MORRISON

## After Being Paralyzed from the Neck down for Twenty Years, Mr. Wallace Gets a Chin-Operated Motorized Wheelchair

For the first time in twenty years
he is mobile, roaring through corridors,
bouncing off walls, out of control,
breaking doorways, tables, chairs,
and regulations. The hallways stretch out
behind him, startled, amazed,
their plaster and wallpaper gaping,
while somewhere far off,
arms spastically flailing,
the small nurses continue to call:
*Mr. Wallace . . . Mr. Wallace . . .*

Eventually he'll listen to reason
and go quietly back to his room,
docile, repentant, and sheepish, promising
not to disappoint them again.
The day shift will sigh and go home.
But, in the evening, between feeding and bedtime,
when they've finally left him alone,
he'll roar over to the corner
and crash through the window
stopping only to watch
the last geese rising,
rising by the light of the snow.

— RONALD WALLACE

## "To: The Access Committee . . ."

"To:
    The Access Committee,
Attention:
    Handicapped Romeo.
        There is now a suitable ramp
installed at my balcony.
        Impatiently,
            Miss Juliet

— H. N. BECKERMAN

## To a Man Going Blind

As you face the evenings
coming on steeper and snowier,
and someone you cannot see
reads in a strained voice
from the book of storms . . .

Dreamlike, a jet climbs
above neighboring houses;
the streets smell
of leafsmoke and gasoline.

Summer was more like a curse
or a scar, the accidental blow
from a man of fire
who carelessly turned toward you
and left his handprint glowing
whitely on your forehead.

All the lamps in your home town
will not light the darkness
growing across a landscape
within you; you wait
like a leaning flower, and hear
almost as if it were nothing,
the petrified rumble
from a world going blind.

— JOHN HAINES

## Black Lightning

A blind girl
stares at me,
then types out ten lines
in braille.

The air has a scent
of sandalwood and
arsenic; a night-blooming cereus
blooms on a dark path.

I look at the
short and long flow
of the lines:
and guess at garlic,
the sun, a silver desert rain,
and palms.

Or is it simply
about hands, a river of light,
the ear of a snail,
or rags?

And, stunned, I feel
the nerves of my hand flashing
in the dark, feel
the world as black
lightning.

— ARTHUR SZE

## The Basket Case

During the war, in high school, I first heard it.
Only a few, the story went, were wounded
so terribly. No stumps to attach
anything to. I imagined it all a lie.

Last night I saw pictures of a man
rigged in an electric harness of levers and arms
and buttons to press with his chin. He ran a business
over the telephone, supported a family,

touched a special typewriter with a stick
held in his teeth. Poured himself a beer.
Strapped in his robot chair, he went to games.
Science and a will to live had given him

the joy that a few years earlier had seemed
impossible. I imagined it all a lie.

— RICHARD FROST

## Brain Tumor

So many live in this town
of intensive care, no one will
recognize your loose mouth,

the one eye that won't close,
the hand that refuses the pen.
Don't worry about the extra step

in the stair, the foyer that bends.
There's no need for the golfball,
the grapefruit-sized bravery—

just hold on. It's someone else,
the one-eyed Joan, who longs
to tell the story: the brain

is an angry man who needed the money,
or the Parthenon, splendid, goat-ridden,
roofless, and blindingly sunny.

— TERESE SVOBODA

## The Steel Plate

They said Mister Dan
Came back from World War II
With a steel plate in his head.
Came back hooked
On Morphine & killed
His need with Muscat.
He came back a hero,
To a ramshackle house
Owned by the Rail Company,
Back to women who came & left
After each government check.

I would close my eyes to see
Metal reflect sunlight
Like a preacher's collection plate.
His tomatoes & sweet corn overtook
The backyard. Peach, plum,
& apricot blossoms deadened
Acid fumes of the papermill.
Fishing poles hung on nails from a wall.
Sometimes I could hear him
Singing a half mile away.
Maybe Creole or German.

But one Saturday he
Was pulled like a moon
Pulls water, dragged naked
Into the midnight street,
Dancing. The next morning
A rain of crushed blossoms
Just wasn't enough to cover
The vaporous smell of human
Feces outside his gate.
His impression in the dirt
Heavier than any white line.

I saw where the police
Blackjacked him to the ground.
Those lilies around that steel-
Gray casket would keep me away
From funerals. Mister Dan's
Dark-brown serge suit . . .
The round plate barely
Beneath a skin of powder
& hair glued into place,
Not able to stop or hide
The sun's gleamy, blue search.

— YUSEF KOMUNYAKAA

## David

David, his glasses,
one clear, one
opaque, lost.
Lost in the parking lot,
Lost walking from one
house to the next.
Lost in the place he knew
this morning, then forgot:

*The sound of water into water,*
*the blue nights, wild,*
*carried to the island, to warmth,*
*to sleep. The sun suddenly*
*a shape on his face, a star of light,*
*then, a leaf on the moon, a blind spot.*

— FRANCINE RINGOLD

## Space

Monday a boy who cannot lift
Even a hand to wave goodbye
Comes to my office with his mother.

She has pushed him in his wheelchair
As she must have bathed and dressed him,
Clipped his beard; knocked on my door.

Now he tries to speak; he sputters.
Leaning down his mother listens,
Nodding at his urgent noises.

Then she tells me that he writes
Using his teeth to punch out letters
One by one, ten hours a page.

"What is he writing?" Yes, he hears me,
Twisting his face while his eyes shine.
"Another novel," his mother says,

"Space is his setting and his theme,
Stars beyond the firmament."
So she talks on. She makes me see

At once the creatures he prefers
Floating across the dreadful night,
Speechless in their metal casing,

Viewing the universe with wonder—
Silent brains, no flesh, no spine—
Amazing in their goodness, pureness.

All the while his lonely eyes
Behold us as we talk and gesture,
Mother, teacher, aliens, stones.

— MAURA STANTON

## Reading a Violent Love Poem to the Deaf

I imagine it's asters the signer
is clenching, their dense centers

long vowels, each a boutonniere
she plants in our lapels.

Delay is what connects me to her—
a lag between speech and gesture

as formal and stately as velvet festoons.
Delay is everything the air burns with,

each crook of her finger
a diacritical spark. I'm seeing legerdemain;

they're seeing American Sign,
a language held like an intricate fan

before the face, but less deceptive.
In the stabbing she mimics, motive

comes clear, the signs cascading
onto the retina so that her song,

drawn on the air, bears its own history,
the love before the knife a wispy

skywriting dissolving before our eyes.
My own hands, clown-sized saboteurs,

betray me with sub-text, as if even
years after I've written these lines

I might reach again for knives
instead of words, when what I want is to leave

the literal entirely, my hands ending in ten
feathers, my mouth a simple net. . . . I pin

my arms to my sides and watch her word roots
shiver into sentences like something shot

in time-lapse—the handshake, maybe, begun
as earnest proof that no weapons

would be used, graduating
into surgery, sculpture, all the ways we sing.

— ENID SHOMER

## Fingers, Fists, Gabriel's Wings

My voice, plucked from the air,
clasped in the interpreter's hands:
fists bloom, close,
pulse of hothouse flowers;
supple fingerpuppet dancers
move to unsounded strains.

Watching the deaf girl listen,
I think there is more to words
than sound ever knows,
brimming handfuls of speech
tempered by secondhand grace.
The word, unutterably, made flesh:
fingers flutter, hover, fold,
the whisk of Gabriel's wings.

— MICHAEL CLEARY

## How to Sign

*Invent* and *father* are said at the forehead.
*Mother* comes out from the chin.
On the bumpy nose sits *fool.*
You won't learn the sign for yes until page 112.
*No* is a beak prattling to its shadow.
In front of the mouth scratches *bird.*
Squeeze the bird once or twice in your hand
to get *orange.* Now you can do anything.
Teach your fingers to spell without you.
Make an island, start a river.
Build a floodgate and walk the width
to let it know your weight.
Test the water with your toes.
Now you can say almost anything.
The line for the past moves back
over the right shoulder.
Stop flailing your arms.
When you finally learn *yes*
it will be a fist knocking.

— LAURIE STROBLAS

## Osteoporosis

FOR MY GRANDMOTHER, LAURA WEINER

Awake, you wonder how to turn,
if your muscles will obey your wishes,
or if the porcelain bones, thinning
with each breath, have grown
insupportable overnight.

At the sink, you pencil in your eyebrows—
mindful of your steady hand, even here
in elderly housing, where the dispossessed
have lost memory,
that transparent muscle.

On Broad Street, trolleys screech and wheeze
like frail men at the back of the synagogue.
Powder. Lipstick. Rouge.
You buckle the brace that trusses
your torso like a dancing partner.

Across the hall, Mr. Weiss fumbles
for his keys. You hear
the knock of his metal walker, three
rubber shoes striking
the floor in a waltz step.

Now you may join the others
in the clamorous dining hall.
Already they are pulling out their chairs,
preparing to recite
the blessing before the meal.

— ROBIN BECKER

## Spastic Child

A silk of flame composed his hair to fleck
His cheeks with freckles dappled on his pallor,
Misplaced like cartoons on a pall, to spatter
His chin laced with a silver thread of spittle
His wax doll hands cannot wipe off. Subsuming
The muted tragedies of moth and mote
Like crucifixes wrought in ivory,
His tongue, slight mollusk broken in its shell,
Is locked so minnows of his wit may never
Leap playing in our waterspouts of words
For the sheer luxury of diving back
Into the pools of quietude, inlaid
With leaves the autumn-umber of his eyes—
His mind, bright bird, forever trapped in silence.

— VASSAR MILLER

## Song for My Son

a wooden puppet with tangled
strings   he bobs and bounces
in mid-air   head flopping
arms waving   my hands
under his arms sustain
his spastic stiffness
the Blue Fairy cradling
sweet Pinocchio

He loves to rock and roll
feet prancing   a crazy
puppet dance   his face glows
with the light   of the wishing
star   and borrowing his
brilliance   we too dance
heads bobbing   arms waving
faster and faster until
cast off puppets all
we fall to the floor   laughing
while the fading light
of the wishing star
caresses his face

— MARILYN DAVIS

# Jenny

You see it's that she can't remember songs
and when friends come to play and want to sing,
you know, songs that children always sing,
she can't remember the songs she sang
even the day before, songs all children sing.

She plays with younger ones,
one little girl really,
and she is so much quicker than my child
and screams at her and calls her stupid
because she can't remember songs.

She can ice skate,
there's nothing wrong with her balance,
and so she glides and looks sad and bewildered
at those who can both skate and sing,
songs that all children know and sing.

And when she is older and the songs are harder
and she needs songs to sing
if she is hurt or loves or isn't sure,
what will she do;
my child who can't remember songs.

— JOHN MANN ASTRACHAN

## Clinics

When I am four a crippled hospital
Peels me out of my parents' arms
To make me better. I wring my mother's neck

For safety, knowing this is not
What they said would happen, that they
Are as unnerved as I am to see
Their mangled only son stripped from their love
Into the cracking-plaster bowels
Of this place, into a row of endless cages
Where children no stronger than their parents'
Worst fears lie writhing, waiting for the legs

The doctors have promised. I have made it
Perfectly clear ever since breakfast
That I want to stop there again on the long
Way back, at that same roadside place
Where I slurped up my hungry hot oats this morning
And they said we'd be sure to, but now
They just stand there growing smaller as some
White-headed woman with her glasses on a chain
Around her neck takes me down the long green
Hallway frowning, and they are still waving goodbye
As we turn the ugly corner and disappear, and what
If I never get my legs and they forget me?

— MICHAEL BACHSTEIN

**Social Issues:**
**Hungry and Frightened by Namelessness**

## Empty Trees

On a summer afternoon
at Bryce Hospital,
the benign are gathered
on the lawn to exercise.

In a ring, counting time,
they touch their toes and raise
their hands above their heads,
up, down, up, down, until

one reaches for the sky and sticks,
fixed in the ancient posture of prayer.
Neither the volunteer who leads them
nor the nurses can make him move.

All winter he watched the trees
empty themselves to embrace.
He knows if he holds out
long enough, he'll be rewarded.

— JACK STEWART

## A Pilgrim of Pilgrims

At 91, cold-cocked on Demerol,
Grandmother basks among the hyacinths,
lost to the stale, sweet pall of Jacksonville,
the lazy river and its hoodlum boats.
My thin aunts squabble like young mockingbirds.
A skeleton among the skeletons,
no blood egg on your finger, the highboy sold,
your cheekbones crazed translucent as onionskin.
The doctors would give you up, have given you up,
your pittance of stock now all utilities
("Natural gas, my dear—what dividends!").
A Kool balancing unlit between your fingers,
the throaty voice of childhood—doomed, not doomed—
calls for the first Scotch and next cigarette.

— WILLIAM LOGAN

## Diminishment

My body
is going away.

It fades
to the transparency
of amber
against the sun.

It shrinks.
It grows quiet.

Small, quiet,
it is a cold
and heavy
smoothed stone.

Who will have it
when it lies
pale and polished
as a clean bone?

— N A N C Y   M A I R S

## Agnes McGurrin

*May your death cause no one pleasure.*—IRISH PROVERB

She can't sleep.
After ten years in a shirt factory
and a marriage of forty years,
after kids, strikes, boredom—
        more kids.
After grandkids, after stroke,
after St. Jude's Home for Diocesan Infirmed,
she can't sleep.
Only this: an image

of late August, a maple losing its leaves.
Her children look consumptive. Thin as twigs.
Here's a table, a bee, a bushel of pears.
They peel easily, smell sweet.
She reaches for a jar and her breasts fall
plump and fragrant into the bushel.
The bee circles her head, Agnes hurries
to finish canning. Her breasts fall again:
pears, more pears . . .
She's flustered, the bee still circling,
then it lights on her wrist. Winter blooms
white as an orchid; a wind stings her awake.

Her husband drops her roughly into the wheelchair
these mornings, and soon he's gone to play cards.
A morning game, pensioners only.
She remembers the club young. Battle of bands.
There was swing, then a slow number.
Lots of smoke and hugging. They'd come early
to see the sand sprinkled on the dance floor.
A handful of sugar to make it smooth.

Agnes starts a letter to her daughter.
She wants to write about *purpose,* but
two cardinals sing from tomato stakes. She's gone
rolling down the wide aisle of her garden.
The birds fly. She begins the ritual
watering, plunging her cupped hand again and again
into the pail, relaxing her fingers over the beans.

Agnes thinks to herself.
A neighbor's phone rings. A bus rumbles past.
She can hardly hear herself,
just a TV preacher voice
through an open window, singing.

— PETER ORESICK

## A Pair of Shoes

This, you were sure, whatever happened,
you'd remember, long as any thought
stuck in your head.
                After a bitter
winter, when you and your family had
to eat weeds, bark, scraps of leather,
and it seemed certain the caked ice
would last forever,
                      the first lull came
drifting over. And then, more sudden
than the dusk invading, a tattered army,
raping, looting, killed all the others,
burned down the huts, and disappeared
before the smoke could scatter.
                          This
you were sure you'd remember, the blood
of your mother soaked in your blouse.

That was how many epochs, how many
countries, earthquakes, holocausts ago?
And oceans washing through, the cloudy
dreams, how many furnished rooms, a rusty
stain on them from how many people?

Now you are old and bent over, old
and bent to this spot called New York.
And crossing the street, only one thing
matters: to keep these broken shoes,
three sizes too big, from falling off.

Beside such chore, your left foot
slowly, slowly sliding after the other,
what a far-off, pointless tale that memory.
Let those sporting a polished pair
which fit indulge themselves.

Crossing
this street, the weight of you collected,
the old blood shuffles through your veins,
too busy to remember.

— THEODORE WEISS

## Alive

Uncle Jimmie had a hunch that cancer,
the rat that gnawed away behind his ears,
was part of the warm earth and silver woods
and snowy meadows in the mountains. Surgeons
stabbed at the rat: scalpels sliced away
the ears one April dawn, as catbirds,
perched in the morning treetops, mocked the calling
of cardinals. Stabbed and missed—the rat survived.
The day they clipped out Uncle Jimmie's cheeks
and upper lip, he pondered artichokes,
truffles, and a certain Tuscan wine.
And when they snipped his nose, he wept for roses
and the fresh sea breeze—and thought a while, and played
his hunch: *Stop cutting,* Jimmie told them, *let
me go to earth and snow and silver trees.*

But the rat kept gnawing, and Auntie Flo went on
reading St. Paul (*The works of the flesh are uncleanness*),
and praying, and paying the bills—and the surgeons huddled,
frowning at Jimmie's want for reverence
for faith and modern medicine. With skillful
suturing, they lifted out his tongue
and dropped the wagging muscle in a pail,
and Uncle Jim, who used to murmur quatrains
out of Omar, kept his peace. Still, his eyes
kept pleading: *Stop the cutting, let me go
to earth and silver trees!* But Jimmie knew
the rat would work in just behind his eyes,
and Auntie Flo would go on reading Paul
(*They that are Christ's have crucified the flesh*)
and praying, and paying the bills—and the pale blue eyes
would have to go: one Sunday after Angelus, Jim began
his dark forgetting of the green
wheat fields, red hills in the sun,
and how the clouds drive storms across the sea.

Some Monday following, a specialist
trimmed away one-quarter of his brain
and left no last gray memory of Omar
or snowy fields      or earth      or silver trees.

But Uncle Jimmie lives: the rat lies quiet now
and tubes lead in and out of Jimmie's veins
and vents. Auntie Flo comes every day
to read to bandages the Word Made Flesh,
and pray, and pay the bills, and watch with Jimmie,
whittled down like a dry stick, but living:
the heart, in its maze of tubes, pumps on,
while catbirds mock the calling of cardinals,
artichokes grow dusty green in sunshine,
butterflies dally with the roses,
and Uncle Jimmie is no part of these.

— PHILIP APPLEMAN

## As Long as You're Happy

IN MEMORY OF RUTH MYERS

I don't know what the Bible says.
My mother who died after being
mercilessly kept alive
by machines at the hospital
looked at the photo of my fiancee
and said, "As long as you're happy . . ."
as if it were the final measure of my reach.

The star through which I shot
my young heart has little value now
except as an occasional reference point,
a piece of cosmic punctuation
some third-rate planet may depend on
to survive.

What I thought was an ethical problem
of existence was just a broken heart.
The woman for whom I have ransomed
my wife and children would like to erase
the past. I would like to gather them all,
please, under one roof, one heart.

About my mother . . .
each day the doctors and machines
said her chances of living
with one more operation
on her overburdened heart
would probably be better.
I thought of reading the Bible then.
It wasn't a question of being happy.

— JACK MYERS

## The Minneapolis Poem

1

I wonder how many old men last winter
Hungry and frightened by namelessness prowled
The Mississippi shore
Lashed blind by the wind, dreaming
Of suicide in the river.
The police remove their cadavers by daybreak
And turn them in somewhere.
Where?
How does the city keep lists of its fathers
Who have no names?
By Nicollet Island I gaze down at the dark water
So beautifully slow.
And I wish my brothers good luck
And a warm grave.

2

The Chippewa young men
Stab one another shrieking
Jesus Christ.
Split-lipped homosexuals limp in terror of assault.
High school backfields search under benches
Near the Post Office. Their faces are the rich
Raw bacon without eyes.
The Walker Art Center crowd stare
At the Guthrie Theater.

3

Tall Negro girls from Chicago
Listen to light songs.
They know when the supposed patron
Is a plainclothesman.
A cop's palm
Is a roach dangling down from the scorched fangs

Of a light bulb.
The soul of a cop's eyes
Is an eternity of Sunday daybreak in the suburbs
Of Juarez, Mexico.

### 4

The legless beggars are gone, carried away
By white birds.
The Artificial Limbs Exchange is gutted
And sown with lime.
The whalebone crutches and hand-me-down trusses
Huddle together dreaming in a desolation
Of dry groins.
I think of poor men astonished to waken
Exposed in broad daylight by the blade
Of a strange plough.

### 5

All over the walls of comb cells
Automobiles perfumed and blindered
Consent with a mutter of high good humor
To take their two naps a day.
Without sound windows glide back
Into dusk.
The sockets of a thousand blind bee graves tier upon tier
Tower not quite toppling.
There are men in this city who labor dawn after dawn
To sell me my death.

### 6

But I could not bear
To allow my poor brother my body to die
In Minneapolis.
The old man Walt Whitman our country man
Is now in America our country
Dead.

But he was not buried in Minneapolis
At least.
And no more may I be
Please God.


7

I want to be lifted up
By some great white bird unknown to the police,
And soar for a thousand miles and be carefully hidden
Modest and golden as one last corn grain,
Stored with the secrets of the wheat and the mysterious lives
Of the unnamed poor.

— JAMES WRIGHT

## County Ward

It begins in a corridor. A woman phones
Her uncle good-bye, the roster for ping-pong
Goes unsigned.
                    It continues,
And Leon naps hugging his shoes.
When he wakens he asks for water,
For rain to come in one door and leave by another;
He asks for the song of a woman
And hears a broom stroke.

Then onto Rachel and Maria, the dull mothers,
Who bandage, sponge dirt from cheeks,
Saying: *Go sleep, baby.*
                    And always
The old one who runs through rooms, cafeteria;
He is a plane watching the horizon
Where his son disappeared.

\*   \*   \*

There is a pain that gets up and moves, like the night attendant,
Pointing to the cough
That rises like dust and is dust
A month later, pointing to the blond one
Who bites a smile and strokes
Under blankets, under the guilt of the one light
That never blinks off.

It comes to speak in the drugged voice
That ate its tongue, the cane tapping
Its way from window to TV,
And back again.
                    Outside,
Left of the neon glowing *Eat,*
Right of the traffic returning home,
This cold slowly deepens

The old whose bones ring with the coming weather,
The black children buttoning and unbuttoning their coats,
The stunned face that could be your father's—
Deepens the gray space between each word
That reaches to say you are alone.

— GARY SOTO

## Veteran's Hospital

WHITE RIVER JUNCTION, VT.

Bringing "only what is needed—essential
toilet articles" in a paper bag,
dressed as for dying, one sees the dying plainly.
These are the homecomings of Agamemnon,
the voyages to the underside of the web
that weaves and unweaves while the suitors gorge upon plenty
and the languishing sons at home unwish their warring
fathers, with strong electric fingers.
                                        The fathers are failing.
In the Hospital Exchange, one sees the dying plainly:
color televisions, beach towels, automatic razors—
the hardware of the affluent society marked
down to cost, to match the negative afflatus
of the ailing, the bandages and badges of their status.
Under the sand-bags, rubber hoses, pipettes, bed-clamps,
tax-exempt, amenable as rabbits,
the unenlisted men are bleeding through their noses
in a perimeter of ramps and apparatus.

In that prosthetic world, the Solarium
lights a junkpile of used parts: the hip that caught
a ricochet of shrapnel; tattoos in curing meats;
scars like fizzled fuses; cancelled postage stamps;
automated claws in candy; the Laser's edge; and barium.
The nurses pass like mowers, dressing and
undressing in the razor-sharp incisions
and the flowering phosphorescence. The smell
of rubbing alcohol rises on desertions and deprivals
and divorces. It is incorruptible. A wheelchair aims
its hospital pajamas like a gun emplacement.
The amputee is swinging in his aviary.
His fingers walk the bird-bars.
                                There is singing
from the Ward-Room—a buzzing of transistors

like blueflies in a urinal. War over war,
the expendables of Metz and Chateau-Thierry,
the guerillas of Bien-Hoa and Korea,
the draftees, the Reserves, the re-enlisters,
open a common wave-length. The catatonic
sons are revving up their combos in the era
of the angry adolescent: their cry is electronic.
Their thumbs are armed with picks. The acid-rock guitarist
in metal studs and chevrons, bombed with magnesium,
mourns like a country yokel, and the innocents
are slaughtered.

       On the terrace, there are juices
and bananas. The convalescent listens to his
heart-beat. The chaplain and his non-combative daughter
smile by the clubbed plants on the portico.

               They shall overcome.

— BEN BELITT

## The Man Stuck between His Shoes

takes a long drink of thunder, lightning, rain
personified as a bird, personified as a car
personified as a wine, liquid bird going down
drinks the stubble of his beard, his body's smell
spreading around him, a blanket no one would trade for
the broken glass he drinks down, the steel cages
of the stores, drinks down the suspicion of eyes
the faces chewing dumpster meals, drinks down
the spaces between houses, the rubble, the empty
windows, the snow dressing what survives, the spreading
disappearance of the East Side, oh, he drinks it all
down, the man holding a knife to his mother's throat
Christmas Eve, the son killing his father, yes, right now
with a baseball bat, the young ones shooting before
they shave, bored with disease, the angry dust
of alleys where no one calls for rags, the hollow
churches turned to missions, the alcoholic ward called
street called bench called crime, the drug ward called
alley called gun called night, and night in day
and he swallows, swallows all till thunder, lightning
rain rise from his throat
no thunderbird, no phoenix.

— JIM DANIELS

## East Washington Street Plasma Center

It pays thirty dollars a visit. The line starts at six.
People who will spend all day searching for aluminum cans
park their supermarket carts up and down the sidewalk.

When they turn on the lights he can see the front desk.
The attendants have papers on him. Every five days
they let him into the white room. He has done this

so many times he could lie there and stick the needle
in his own arm. The rest is easy. They drain a pint
of something out of him, but he does not believe

it is really blood, because they always put back
as much as they take out. They have told him
about plasma, shown him the centrifuge whirling,

even pointed out the place on the map where it goes:
somewhere in southern California. They do not realize
that he controls things with his mind. Part of him stays

in California, inside other people, having a good time,
going to the track every day, winning, sending money home
to pay for more plasma. The other part is invisible,

it gets loose, there are people out looking for it,
trying to find it, but in five days it comes back,
all that way, and he is ready to go inside again.

— JARED CARTER

## The Addict

Sleepmonger,
deathmonger,
with capsules in my palms each night,
eight at a time from sweet pharmaceutical bottles
I make arrangements for a pint-sized journey.
I'm the queen of this condition.
I'm an expert on making the trip
and now they say I'm an addict.
Now they ask why.
Why!

Don't they know
that I promised to die!
I'm keeping in practice.
I'm merely staying in shape.
The pills are a mother, but better,
every color and as good as sour balls.
I'm on a diet from death.

Yes, I admit
it has gotten to be a bit of a habit—
blows eight at a time, socked in the eye,
hauled away by the pink, the orange,
the green and the white goodnights.
I'm becoming something of a chemical
mixture.
That's it!

My supply
of tablets
has got to last for years and years.
I like them more than I like me.
Stubborn as hell, they won't let me go.
It's a kind of marriage.

It's a kind of war
where I plant bombs inside
of myself.

Yes
I try
to kill myself in small amounts,
an innocuous occupation.
Actually I'm hung up on it.
But remember I don't make too much noise.
And frankly no one has to lug me out
and I don't stand there in my winding sheet.
I'm a little buttercup in my yellow nightie
eating my eight loaves in a row
and in a certain order as in
the laying on of hands
or the black sacrament.

It's a ceremony
but like any other sport
it's full of rules.
It's like a musical tennis match where
my mouth keeps catching the ball.
Then I lie on my altar
elevated by the eight chemical kisses.

What a lay me down this is
with two pink, two orange,
two green, two white goodnights.
Fee-fi-fo-fum—
Now I'm borrowed.
Now I'm numb.

— ANNE SEXTON

## Literal

All those flourishes and curlicues were his
best irrepressibility—each letter
traced in the air with a toetip, each fine
detail of trill in the gardened uprush.
Hollows needed him
in order to resound—there he began
to spin his hammock out
of palm and text and unspent sex.

And then he got so sick
he couldn't get from bed.
The sheet was signed with shit and he himself
at thirty-seven, stricken by that fact,
was hexed by people's kisses, vexed by people's energies,
the very wrath of ornament turned on
itself, its former favorite.
Finally he dropped the chromosome bible,
cared no more for calligraphic nature,
x's of treasure or animal track.
Death moved him, far
from laughter, far from figured lights and darks and far
from foreign and familiar time. I left his house
and walked among the monuments, in parks.

And that was when I saw the ferns—
arising everywhere from warmish ground,
promiscuously pale, preeminently question-marks.

— HEATHER MCHUGH

## In the Waiting Room

St. Gaudens would have known what would suit
this research institution: a tall,
stately figure of Science, proudly
undeterred, her plain draperies hung
in even rows to soften the cast
of her bronze body, one hand aloft
raising a hypodermic needle.

Before such images these six-month
check-ups would seem like a pilgrimage
in which unpardonable clerics
and unbathed wives had walked before me.
But in this vast, unadorned building
there's no distraction from my purpose
or the object for which I've journeyed.

With only the pages of *People*
and *Time* for amusement, who would not
feel afraid? For I am here as part
of a study on the life cycle
of the adult homosexual,
to see which of us will sicken next
in our group of twelve hundred odd

from this strange disease of yet unknown
beginnings that teaches the body
how to betray the life within it.
An endangered species, we are watched
to see how it makes its first appearance
and all the stages on which it acts
in our theatre of operations.

Sometimes two or three men are waiting
to be called—not by name—but number
to preserve our anonymity

(though who in the face of such cool
clinical detachment could retain
a sense of self?). Yet at times one might
see a friend or distant acquaintance

head down or looking at the wall
(there are no windows here) marking where
the plaster has given way. I stop,
exchange a few meaningless phrases
and perhaps he'll have a joke to tell
or news or someone known in common
until the silence descends once more.

And once, early for my appointment,
I was left alone when voices shot
through swinging doors. A man in a white
laboratory coat and another
clad in jeans were speaking, and I knew
that the man in denim had become
the person I feared that I might be.

And I hated him for having brought
his death so near that I could touch it,
and the room seemed to fill with the dread
odor of his dying, and I sat amazed:
for with his neat beard and curly hair
and the whiteness of his freckled face,
he might be taken for my lover.

Now the two were arguing in that
complicitous tone of handymen
faced with a machine that will not work.
What about this? Or that? they question,
uncertain which, if any, repairs
to undertake, running their cold hands
along the ailing anatomy.

"I'll never live through *that*," the patient
laughs, as though it were another's case
he were discussing. I asked myself,
can this be true? Can people withdraw
so far from their existence that life
and death become academic games
left to pique their curiosity,

a trivial pursuit that will not
bore when played for hours at a time?
Or is there some catharsis unknown
to me, when what you fear will happen
happens and there's nothing more to fear,
and one reaches that calm meadow where
the sacred few are allowed to rest

beyond the walled, polluted city
that cast them out? They are gone away
now out of sight through another set
of fire doors, but their voices still
can be heard faintly like a new spring
or the hushed tones of lovers careful
not to wake the disapproving crowd.

A nurse approaches, clipboard in hand.
Have I brought my paraphernalia,
samples of semen and excrement
which the study cannot do without?
And the old terror revives in me
of what they will find: the truth, perhaps,
that I like everyone else will die.

Bring him back, bring him back, the one who
gave me his healing touch. I'm ready
to embrace him now if he can stop
the pain of losing what was never
mine to keep. Bring him back

so that he can teach me how to be
content when I take his place at last.

— DAVID BERGMAN

## Elegy for John, My Student Dead of AIDS

In my office, where you sat years ago and talked
Of Donne, of how you loved
His persona, the bravado he could muster
To cover love's uncertainties,
Books still line the shelves, centuries
Of writers who've tried to make a kind of sense
Of life and death and, failing that,
Found words to stand at least
Against the griefs we can't resolve.

Now you're dead. And what I've got to say
Comes now from that silence
When our talk last fouled up. I allowed you less,
As always, than you wanted to say.
We talked beside the Charles, a lunch hour reunion
Of sorts after years of your postcards
(New York, San Francisco, Greece),
Failed attempts to find a place to live.
The warm weather had come on

In a rush. You talked of being the first born,
Dark-haired, Italian son. How you rarely visited
The family you so clearly loved.
I shifted to books, to sunlight falling
Through sycamores and the idle play of underlying
Shadows. When we parted,
All that was really left was the feeling
You deserved better. And yet I was relieved
Our hour was up, that we had kept your confusion

To yourself. We shook hands, you drove off to Boston.
Now you're dead and I wonder
If your nobleness of living with no one
To turn to ended in dishonor,
Your family ashamed. Or if your death had

About it a frail dignity,
Each darkening bruise precise as a writer's word,
Saying, at last who you were—exactly
And to anyone who would listen.

— ROBERT CORDING

## Tarantula or The Dance of Death

During the plague I came into my own.
It was a time of smoke-pots in the house
Against infection. The blind head of bone
      Grinned its abuse

Like a good democrat at everyone.
Runes were recited daily, charms were applied.
That was the time I came into my own.
      Half Europe died.

The symptoms are a fever and dark spots
First on the hands, then on the face and neck,
But even before the body, the mind rots.
      You can be sick

Only a day with it before you're dead.
But the most curious part of it is the dance.
The victim goes, in short, out of his head.
      A sort of trance

Glazes the eyes, and then the muscles take
His will away from him, the legs begin
Their funeral jig, the arms and belly shake
      Like souls in sin.

Some, caught in these convulsions, have been known
To fall from windows, fracturing the spine.
Others have drowned in streams. The smooth head-stone,
      The box of pine,

Are not for the likes of these. Moreover, flame
Is powerless against contagion.
That was the black winter when I came
      Into my own.

— ANTHONY HECHT

## The Eulogy

The man in the black suit delivers a eulogy
each page he turns, turns
a page of light on the ceiling,

because death mimics us, mocking
the eye's cowardly flight
from the flower-covered coffin

to the framed photo of the bereaved, alive.
It is not night.
It is California.

There are hibiscus dropping
their veined shrouds
on the crushed-stone path outside.

A gold cuff link blazes
as the eulogist raises his hands.

Shadows alter the ceiling,
the readable text.
*There are two ways to meet death,*

he says. One fearful,
the other courageous.
One day purposeful, the next hopeless.

A young man died because he had sex.
The eulogist speaks of soldiers under fire,
the cowards and the heroes.

The woman next to me cannot stop
weeping. I can find no tears inside
me. The cuff links beam

signals at us, above us.
The sun through the skylight
grows brighter and brighter:

Watch now, God,
Watch the eulogist raise his hands.
The rays, like your lasers,

blind the front rows.
The gifts love gives us!
Some of us flinch, some do not.

— CAROL MUSKE

## On Market Street

in front of the department store,
in the full surprise of day,
a young girl is lying
on a white-sheeted hospital bed.

At first there is only
the fact of her, an impediment
to be gotten around
like a statue or accident.

But I'm stopped by the arms that end
in dull blades, the stiffness
of the form under the sheet.

Dust and sun drift down to her.
I watch her eyes fill up with light.
Then, as if she'd beckoned them,
the heavy-footed pigeons come.

How calm she is, like a painted saint,
like a miracle she is used to.
Someone throws money in the cardboard box
a woman holds. A small boy, too,

is hovering nearby. She
is theirs. They are glad for her.
Anyone would be, seeing their hopes,
though they twist, come to some use.

They bear her along
as if all the souls in the world
corresponded in number to the stars,
each in its own vehicle.

— ELAINE TERRANOVA

## There Now

He wasn't himself, your father.
Even your mother couldn't rouse him,
even to the old arguments.
So the toast was cold?

The room was cold where he burned
at sea in their old bed,
like some small craft turned on its side,
spars bony under a clammy sail.

Six cigarettes a day the doctor allowed.
One burned neglected, its bedside vigil
capsized into a mere breath of ash.
Your mother lit another.

His pale hands barely touched his pale food
as if already he were beyond all this
although he'd not been told how ill he was.
Could he not have known?

Already he had the cast of a northern saint,
one so pale he still glows under the dust
that is the long history of forgetfulness.
One who holds a small building

Like a baby forever toward us
whose attentions soon turn elsewhere,
to love or lunch, the tarnished leaf
of grace falling but never touching us.

The ocean sinks into its salt
or we rise above it, the plane torn
between the gravity of human wishes
and cloud spun from airy nothing—

these white loaves, the whiter fish drifted
from the deep blue a miniaturist filled in
behind some unconvincing rocks
floating a far-off frill of waves

stitched to a little gash of boat,
a saint standing around, hands full,
looking cold and a little lost.
And then we, too, are above it all,

the earth bandaged with cotton wool.
*There,* your mother would say in promise
of great distance from a little crescent
of scar. *There now. There, there.*

— DEBORA GREGER

## Old Women

> . . . *little packages, oh yes,*
> *all old women make little packages*
> *and stow them under their beds.*
> —JOSÉ DONOSO, THE OBSCENE BIRD OF NIGHT

Evidence of *a woman's hard life*
on faces lined with meaning
like the Rosetta Stone; a litany
of ailments, marks of fear, nights of pain, knowledge
of solitude, of shameful family secrets,
and the occasional ecstasy they dare you to decipher.

Stored under groaning mattresses are the remnants
of their lives wrapped in little packages, taped or
tied with string: wedding photos
jaundiced with age and humidity, of couples
standing stiff as corpses at the greatest distance
the frame will allow, of serious infants
held by women in severe dresses. In bundles,
sheaves of magazines becoming

one moist lump; balls of string, baby clothes of cracked satin
and ragged lace, shoes curling tongue-to-heel—homogenized,
all of it velvety to the touch,
turning in the thick air of wet coughs and tea,
the thing they all once were—paper to pulp, cloth to fiber,
ashes to ashes.

Old women sit like hens over their soft bundles,
nest and nursery of their last days, letting
the effluence of memory, its pungent odor
of decay work through the clogged channels
of their brains, presiding over their days
like an opium dream.

— JUDITH ORTIZ COFER

## Near the Old People's Home

The people on the avenue at noon,
Sharing the sparrows and the wintry sun,
The turned-off fountain with its basin drained
And cement benches etched with checkerboards,

Are old and poor, most every one of them
Wearing some decoration of his damage,
Bandage or crutch or cane; and some are blind,
Or nearly, tap-tapping along with white wands.

When they open their mouths, there are no teeth.
All the same, they keep on talking to themselves
Even while bending to hawk up spit or blood
In gutters that will be there when they are gone.

Some have the habit of getting hit by cars
Three times a year; the ambulance comes up
And away they go, mumbling even in shock
The many secret names they have for God.

— HOWARD NEMEROV

## The Very Old

The very old are forever
hurting themselves,

burning their fingers
on skillets, falling

loosely as trees
and breaking their hips

with muffled explosions of bone.
Down the block

they are wheeled in
out of our sight

for years at a time.
To make conversation,

the neighbors ask
if they are still alive.

Then, early one morning,
through our kitchen windows

we see them again,
first one and then another,

out in their gardens
on crutches and canes,

perennial,
checking their gauges for rain.

— TED KOOSER

## The Social Impact of Corporate Disinvestment

Pittsburgh, Toledo, Chicago, Detroit.
Uncle Paul changed mills like shoes,
Aunt Sophie dragging behind, dragging
their six weepy daughters.
He ended finally in Kansas, in General Motors,
where his bad heart caught up to him.

My cousins called the priest,
the undertaker, and the doctor,
who gave Sophie a little something.
It was November then.
The stars could barely shine
through the Presbyterian heavens.
Somehow desire, like a cyclone,
swept over the prairie, over her flat life,
confused her.
                                She walked out
naked into a field beyond the garage.
Threw herself flat.
Embraced the earth without a tear.

The sun had long since risen
by the time she returned home.
"Mother!" they all wailed, and promptly
put her to bed, pale and waxen.
The priest was summoned.

When he had finished the prayer
of the dying over her, she sat up,
quite cheerful, and from her pillow
withdrew a ten. His stipend.
They all looked at each other and looked
at each other—and drifted to the kitchen
for the poppy seed and nut rolls and coffee.

— PETER ORESICK

## The Ones That Are Thrown Out

One has flippers. This one is like a seal.
One has gills. This one is like a fish.
One has webbed hands, is like a duck.
One has a little tail, is like a pig.
One is like a frog
with no dome at all above the eyes.

They call them bad babies.

They didn't mean to be bad
but who does.

— MILLER WILLIAMS

## The Retarded Children Find a World
## Built Just for Them

The doors of that city are ninety feet high,
On their panels are frescoes of ships, of mountains.

Inside is the children's kingdom
Where the mad ones, the foot-draggers, garglers,

Askew as a tower of beads,
Are sustained by the air. Buildings, like great gold chains

Emboss themselves around
The crazy children, their jewels.

The children turn and turn like dancers,
Their sweaters whirl out at their waists, their long chopped hair

Scrapes the side of the archways,
They're happy, they're famous.

They walk on the streets in crystal shoes, lapis flows in the gutters;
Around the edge of each building there's a scarlet halo.

And those children with eyes like scars, with tongues sewed to the
                    roofs of their palates, with hands that jerk

Like broken-backed squirrels,
Feed the writing of light from the buildings;

They forgive us ninety times over;
They sing and sing like all the birds of the desert.

— DIANA O'HEHIR

## Of a Night Fed with No Forgetfulness

The war never stops making holes.

15 years after Saigon and still you bolt awake.
I listen to leaves scrape against glass.
You hear in the throat of all that stirs
a blind animal noise. You wrap yourself up
in arms, cradling again a Tommy pitched
like a cinder out of a six helicopter collision.
You see orange light gushing black smoke.
Orders bellow to "forget what you can't save."
Legs gone, he lay crumpled in the hospital
hallway, a lump of coal, cast off to be tagged.
You stopped to sponge his eyes blistered shut.
His lips squeaked, "Somebody help me die."
You lifted the charred stump of him
into your arms and rocked to sleep his ashes
with needle after needle of nurse's morphine.
Your eyes sear into my shoulder, two bright holes.
"I'm scared," they say. "Nothing will go away."

— J. P. WHITE

## The Prisoner

FOR AMNESTY INTERNATIONAL

Bowing before boot & fist
you learn to hide

small hands in sleep
& flee in terror like a child

from the pain that makes you
human. Soon hour of the

"blue lit stage" when
you will open like a rose

before blind operators
& their machines—"a telephone."

It will be a birthday party
with tea & burnt toast

where you will star—stranger
holding the heavy stone,

tarantula rattling
bamboo bars—each betraying

scream gagged by shit
in a paper bag. Left you

will be these little
miracles—*corragio*

in a matchbox, a song
carried faintly on the wind,

scent of periwinkles &
black drink of oblivion.

— L. S. ASEKOFF

## Simple Truths

When a man has grown a body,
a body to carry with him
through nature for as long as he can,
when this body is taken from him
by other men and women who happen to be,
this time, in uniform,
then it is clear he has experienced
an act of barbarism,

and when a man has a wife,
a wife to love for as long as he lives,
when this wife is marked with a yellow star
and driven into a chamber she will never leave alive,
then this is murder,
so much is clear,

and when a woman has hair,
when her hair is shorn and her scalp bleeds,
when a woman has children,
children to love for as long as she lives,
when the children are taken from her,
when a man and his wife and their children
are put to death in a chamber of gas,
or with pistols at close range, or are starved,
or beaten, or injected by the thousands,
or ripped apart, by the thousands, by the millions,

it is clear that where we are
is Europe, in our century, during the years
from nineteen-hundred and thirty-five
to nineteen-hundred and forty-five
after the death of Jesus, who spoke of a different order,
but whose father, who is our father,
if he is our father,

if we must speak of him as father,
watched, and witnessed, and knew,

and when we remember,
when we touch the skin of our own bodies,
when we open our eyes into dream
or within the morning shine of sunlight
and remember what was taken
from these men, from these women,
from these children gassed and starved
and beaten and thrown against walls
and made to walk the valley
of knives and icepicks and otherwise
exterminated in ways appearing to us almost
beyond even the maniacal human imagination,
then it is clear that this is the German Reich,
during approximately ten years of our lord's time,

and when we read a book of these things,
when we hear the names of the camps,
when we see the films of the bulldozed dead
or the film of one boy struck on the head
with a club in the hands
of a German doctor who will wait
some days for the boy's skull to knit, and will enter
the time in his ledger, and then
take up the club to strike the boy again,
and wait some weeks for the boy's skull to knit,
and enter the time in his ledger again,
and strike the boy again,
and so on, until the boy, who,
at the end of the film of his life
can hardly stagger forward toward the doctor,
does die, and the doctor
enters exactly the time of the boy's death in his ledger,

when we read these things or see them,
then it is clear to us that this
happened, and within the lord's allowance, this
work of his minions, his poor
vicious dumb German victims twisted
into the swastika shapes of trees struck by lightning,
on this his earth, if he is our father,
if we must speak of him in this way,
this presence above us, within us, this
mover, this first cause, this spirit, this
curse, this bloodstream and brain-current, this
unfathomable oceanic ignorance of ourselves, this
automatic electric Aryan swerve, this

fortune that you and I were not the victims, this
luck that you and I were not the murderers, this
sense that you and I are clean and understand, this
stupidity that gives him breath, gives him life
as we kill them all, as we killed them all.

— WILLIAM HEYEN

# Elegy

He went without a cry or a kick,
a blink or a hic. From one sleep, he
slipped into another. Gently
he turned in his fluid existence
until the liquid globe became his
singular struggle and he shifted

the great weight of being. Thus, he was
free from all lessons, languages, and
love. By being less than five hundred
grams of unborn dreams, he escaped
each legislation. Missing even
the morgue, he lay in a bucket where

he was cradled in his circular
fate. To a brain with a microscope,
he donated his bean-sized kidneys;
sticks of bone marrow he bequeathed
to the soul of science. He gave new
flesh to fire and softened the ashes

with innocence. A frenzy of white
spirits, flocking like gulls, gathered
his ghost. He was so unassuming
doing his dervish of life and death,
so lusty in his liberation
so lost to reconciliation.

— SUSAN KINSOLVING

## Abortion

Coming home, I find you still in bed,
but when I pull back the blanket,
I see your stomach is flat as an iron.
You've done it, as you warned me you would
and left the fetus wrapped in wax paper
for me to look at. My son.
Woman, loving you no matter what you do,
what can I say, except that I've heard
the poor have no children, just small people
and there is room for only one man in this house.

— A I

## The Nursing Home

When we took the Hershey bar
to Aunt Edris in the nursing home
she was still alert enough to say
"Don't leave it there,
they'll steal it. They steal
most everything. They got
my rings, they got my locket too."
So we shared it out, a kind
of communion, chocolate on her tongue,
ours. The only thing
they had no use for
was the stack of yellowed snapshots,
for which we thank
the not quite heartless thief.

— DAVID RAY

## Accident

Decerebrated, a hole cut in your neck
the size of a quarter, you can only breathe and then,
only if I keep your trachea clean, hourly suction
the green strings of mucus that plug over the hole.
I go down and down with the metal-tipped catheter
until finally it pulls nothing back. You gag, choke,
turn blue and I click off the machine.

One arm stretches above your head, elbow flattened
and turned out; the other lies extended along
your hip and thigh and the fingers of your hands
are clenched as if they hold on to all you own.
All I know about you is this animal posturing,
the feel of your loose muscles when I turn you,
the steamy smell of machines pumping constantly
around your bed and that whole sections
of your brain are gone, lost in the minutes
you lay anoxic, waiting for someone to find you,
waiting for a stranger's fist
to beat your heart back alive.

He slammed on his brakes when he saw your motorcycle
crushed against the guard-rail, then saw the blood
congealed on your clothes, streamed from your mouth
across your cheek to your ear. He felt no pulse
on your damp neck. You look so young, even less
than twenty-five. What did he think, seeing you?
He had to save you, adrenalin so sprung
he never thought to check your pupils, never
thought how long you might have waited
and he saved you.

— KARIN T. ASH

## A Twenty-Four-Week Preemie, Change of Shift

We're running out of O$_2$
screaming down the southwest freeway in the rain
the nurse-practitioner and me
rocking around in the back of an ambulance
trying to ventilate a preemie with junk for lungs
when we hit
rush hour

      *Get us the hell out of here*

*You bet* the driver said and pulled right onto the median strip
with that maniacal glee they get

I was too scared for the kid and drunk with the speed
the danger—that didn't feel like danger at all
it felt like love—to worry about *my* life
Fuck that

*Get us back to Children's so we can put a chest tube in this kid*

And when we got to the unit
the attending physician—Loretta—was there
and the nurses
and the residents
they save us
Loretta plants her stethoscope on the kid's chest
and here comes the tech driving the portable X-ray
like it's a Porsche—*Ah Jesus* he says
the baby's so puny he could fit on your dinner plate

*X-ray* says the tech
and everybody backs up, way back
except for Loretta
so the tech drapes a lead shield over her chest

*X-ray* says the tech

There's a moment after he cones down the lens
just before he shoots
you hold your breath, you forget
what's waiting
back at your house

Nobody blinks
poised for that sound that radiological
*meep*

and Loretta with her scrub top on backwards
so you can't peep down to her peanutty boobs
Loretta with her half-Chinese, half-Trinidadian
half-smile
Loretta, all right, ambu-bagging the kid
never misses a beat
calm and sharp as a mama-cat who's kicked the dog's butt
now softjaws her kitten out of the ditch

There's a moment
you can't even hear the bag
puffing
quick quick quick
before the tech shoots
for just that second
I quit being scared
I forget to be scared

God

How can people abandon each other?

— BELLE WARING

## Secret Places of Forrest Lane

Forsythia was a low arcade, a lair
where tendril-branches cast themselves aside
over and over again, gold-studded flowers
in coppery green hair.
A useful place to hide
whenever the fighting hit a certain pitch
or simmered, tight or sober as my father.
My mother did what women usually do
before they draw the line: dissemble, plead,
scold and compensate and throw out bottles.
None of it helps. The drinker has to drown
in his own cups before he comes around,
if he wants to live enough. My father did.

After torrential snows
that flattened the forsythia and dogwood,
after the summer floods that made our lane
a small canal and killed the cellar pump,
after a series of blind catastrophes
that seemed like great adventure to a child
and trouble to my parents,
inspired or terrified, my father quit.

When I crept out of hiding, he was there,
though half-transparent, like an earthly cloud.
Gentle and self-occluded, self-enclosed,
but there. So my young parents ceased to fight
and picked up wiser habits,
inventing my two brothers by surprise.
The township widened Forrest Lane so firmly
the border of forsythia disappeared.
I learned to live without it, now and then
finding my heart a better place to hide.

— EMILY GROSHOLZ

## Death Psalm: O Lord of Mysteries

She   grew old.
She   made ready to die.
She   gave counsel to women and men, to young girls and
                                      young boys.
She   remembered her griefs.
She   remembered her happinesses.
She   watered the garden.
She   accused herself.
She   forgave herself.
She   learned new fragments of wisdom.
She   forgot old fragments of wisdom.
She   abandoned certain angers.
She   gave away gold and precious stones.
She   counted-over her handkerchiefs of fine lawn.
She   continued to laugh on some days, to cry on others,
                  unfolding the design of her identity.
She   practiced the songs she knew, her voice
                         gone out of tune
            but the breathing pattern perfected.
She   told her sons and daughters she was ready.
She   maintained her readiness.
She   grew very old.
She   watched the generations increase.
She   watched the passing of seasons and years.
She   did not die.

She   did not die but lies half-speechless, incontinent,
            aching in body, wandering in mind
            in a hospital room.
A plastic tube, taped to her nose,
      disappears into one nostril.
Plastic tubes are attached to veins in her arms.
Her urine runs through a tube into a bottle under the bed.
On her back and ankles are black sores.
The   black sores are parts of her that have died.

The   beat of her heart is steady.
She   is not whole.
She   made ready to die, she prayed, she made her peace,
        she read daily from the lectionary.
She   tended the green garden she had made,
        she fought off the destroying ants,
        she watered the plants daily
        and took note of their blossoming.
She   gave sustenance to the needy.
She   prepared her life for the hour of death.
But   the hour has passed and she has not died.

O Lord of mysteries, how beautiful is sudden death
        when the spirit vanishes
        boldly and without casting
        a single shadowy feather of hesitation
        onto the felled body.

O Lord of mysteries, how baffling, how clueless
        is laggard death, disregarding
        all that is set before it
            in the dignity of welcome—
laggard death, that steals
            insignificant patches of flesh—
laggard death, that shuffles
past the open gate,
past the open hand,
past the open,
            ancient,
            courteously awaiting life.

— DENISE LEVERTOV

## Lullaby

Each morning I finish my coffee,
And climb the stairs to the charts,
Hoping yours will be filed away.
But you can't hear me,
You can't see yourself clamped
Between this hard plastic binder:
Lab reports and nurses' notes, a sample
In a test tube. I keep reading
These terse comments: stable as before,
Urine output still poor, respiration normal.
And you keep on poisoning
Yourself, your kidneys more useless
Than seawings drenched in an oil spill.
I find my way to your room
And lean over the bedrails
As though I can understand
Your wheezed-out fragments.
What can I do but check
Your tubes, feel your pulse, listen
To your heartbeat insistent
As a spoiled child who goes on begging?

Old man, listen to me:
Let me take you in a wheelchair
To the back room of the records office,
Let me lift you in my arms
And lay you down in the cradle
Of a clean manila folder.

— JON MUKAND

# Permissions

In order to obtain current copyright information, the editor has attempted in every instance to contact the author or the publisher of the poems included in this collection. In some cases, however, such information may still be incomplete. The copyright to each individual work remains with the author or other copyright holder as designated by the author.

*Blue Like the Heavens*, University of Pittsburgh Press, 1984. Reprinted by permission of the author.

Patricia Goedicke: "One More Time" from *The Tongues We Speak, New and Selected Poems*, Milkweed Editions, copyright 1989 by Patricia Goedicke. Reprinted by permission of the author.

Albert Goldbarth: "Edgewater Hospital" from *Poetry*, reprinted in *Faith*, New Rivers Press, copyright 1981 by Albert Goldbarth. Reprinted by permission of the author.

Debora Greger: "There Now" copyright 1994 by Debora Greger. Reprinted by permission of the author.

Eamon Grennan: "Diagnosis" from *As If It Matters*, Graywolf Press, 1992. Reprinted by permission of the author.

Emily Grosholz: "In the Light of October" from *The River Painter*, University of Illinois Press, 1984. "Secret Places of Forrest Lane" from *Eden*, Johns Hopkins University Press, 1992. Reprinted by permission of the author and the publisher.

Pamela White Hadas: "To Make a Dragon Move: From the Diary of an Anorexic" from *Beside Herself: Pocahontas to Patty Hearst*, Knopf, copyright 1983 by Pamela White Hadas. Reprinted by permission of the author.

Rachel Hadas: "Upon My Mother's Death" from *Pequod*, copyright 1993 by Rachel Hadas. Reprinted by permission of the author.

Susan Hahn: "Agoraphobia" and "Claustrophobia" from *Harriet Rubin's Mother's Wooden Hand*, University of Chicago Press, 1991. Reprinted by permission of the publisher.

John Haines: "To a Man Going Blind" copyright 1971 by John Haines. Reprinted by permission of the author and Graywolf Press.

Jim Hall: "Tennis Elbow" from *Poetry*, May 1986. Reprinted by permission of the author.

Judith Hall: "Malignancies in Winter" previously published, in somewhat different form, in *13th Moon*, 1984. Reprinted by permission of the author.

Jeffrey Harrison: "For a Friend in the Hospital" from *The Singing Underneath*, copyright 1988 by Jeffrey Harrison. Reprinted by permission of Dutton Signet, a division of Penguin Books USA.

William Harrold: "Putting Them Down" copyright 1994 by William Harrold. Reprinted by permission of the author.

Lola Haskins: "A Note on the Acquisition by American Medical

from *Sure Signs: New and Se-
lected Poems*, University of Pitts-
burgh Press, copyright 1980 by
Ted Kooser. Reprinted by permis-
sion of the publisher. "The Very
Old" from *One World at a Time*,
University of Pittsburgh Press,
copyright 1985 by Ted Kooser.
Reprinted by permission of the
publisher.

Maxine Kumin: "Rehabilitation
Center" from *Halfway*, Holt,
Rinehart & Winston, copyright
1961 by Maxine Kumin. Re-
printed by permission of the
author.

David Lanier: "Night Watch" copy-
right 1994 by David Lanier.
Printed by permission of the
author.

Sydney Lea: "The Return: Intensive
Care" from *New Yorker*, reprinted
in *No Sign*, University of Georgia
Press, copyright 1987 by Sydney
Lea. Reprinted by permission of
the author.

Rika Lesser: "Shocking Treatment"
from the Tenth Anniversary Issue
of the *George Washington Re-
view*, to be reprinted in *All We
Need of Hell*, University of North
Texas Press, 1995. Reprinted by
permission of the author.

Denise Levertov: "Talking to Grief"
and "Death Psalm: O Lord of
Mysteries" from *Life in the For-
est*, copyright 1978 by Denise

Levertov. Reprinted by per-
mission of New Directions
Publishing.

Philip Levine: "The Doctor of Star-
light" from *One for the Rose*,
Atheneum, copyright 1981 by
Philip Levine. Reprinted by per-
mission of the author.

William Logan: "A Pilgrim of Pil-
grims" copyright 1994 by William
Logan. Printed by permission of
the author.

Thomas Lux: "Hospital View" from
*Half Promised Land*, Houghton
Mifflin, 1986. Reprinted by per-
mission of the author.

Marcia Lynch: "Peau d'Orange"
reprinted by permission of the
author.

Norman MacCaig: "Visiting Hour"
from *Collected Poems*, Chatto &
Windus. Reprinted by permission
of Random House UK Limited.

Cynthia MacDonald: "In Such an
Unhappy Neighborhood, Carlos"
from *Living Wills: New and Se-
lected Poems*, Knopf, copyright
1991 by Cynthia MacDonald. Re-
printed by permission of the
author.

Heather McHugh: "Literal" from
*Hinge & Sign: New and Selected
Poems*, Wesleyan University
Press, copyright 1994 by Heather
McHugh. Reprinted by permis-
sion of the author.

Sandra McPherson: "Pregnancy"

*certainties and Rest,* copyright 1994 by Timothy Steele. Reprinted by permission of the author.

Gerald Stern: "Love for the Dog" from *The Red Coal,* Houghton Mifflin, copyright by Gerald Stern. Reprinted by permission of the author.

Jack Stewart: "Empty Trees" copyright 1994 by Jack Stewart. Printed by permission of the author.

John Stone: "Amnesia," "Getting to Sleep in New Jersey," and "To a 14 Year Old Girl in Labor and Delivery" from *The Smell of Matches,* Rutgers University Press, 1972. Reprinted by permission of the author.

Marc Straus: "A Pause" and "Questions and Answers" copyright 1994 by Marc Straus. Printed by permission of the author.

Laurie Stroblas: "How to Sign" from *Toward Solomon's Mountain,* Temple University Press, 1986, copyright by Laurie Stroblas. Reprinted by permission of the author.

Lucien Stryk: "Voyage" from *American Poetry Review,* January/February 1993. Reprinted by permission of the author.

Amber Coverdale Sumrall: "A Question of Energy" from *Toward Solomon's Mountain,* Temple University Press, 1986. Reprinted by permission of the publisher.

Terese Svoboda: "Brain Tumor" copyright 1994 by Terese Svoboda. Reprinted by permission of the author.

Cole Swensen: "Electrocardiogram" copyright 1994 by Cole Swensen. Printed by permission of the author.

Arthur Sze: "Black Lightning" from *Dazzled,* copyright 1982 by Arthur Sze. Reprinted by permission of the author.

James Tate: "On the Subject of Doctors" from *Viper Jazz,* Wesleyan University Press, 1976, copyright by James Tate. Reprinted by permission of the author.

Henry Taylor: "Frank Amos and the Way Things Work" from *New Virginia Review,* copyright 1986 by Henry Taylor. Reprinted by permission of the author.

Elaine Terranova: "On Market Street" from *The Cult of the Right Hand,* Doubleday, 1991. Reprinted by permission of the author.

Richard Tillinghast: "For a Teacher's Wife, Dying of Cancer" copyright 1994 by Richard Tillinghast. Reprinted by permission of the author.

Constance Urdang: "Birth" and

"Change of Life" from *The Lone Woman and Others*, University of Pittsburgh Press, 1980. Reprinted by permission of the author and the publisher.

Mona Van Duyn: "In the Hospital for Tests" from *To See, To Take*, Atheneum, 1971. Reprinted by permission of the author.

Doris Vidaver: "Vita Brevis" from *Chicago Tribune Magazine*, 1993, copyright by Doris Vidaver. Reprinted by permission of the author.

Ellen Bryant Voigt: "Damage" from *Claiming Kin*, Wesleyan University Press, copyright by Ellen Bryant Voigt. Reprinted by permission of the author.

David Wagoner: "On Seeing an X-ray of My Head" from *Collected Poems*, Indiana University Press, copyright 1976 by David Wagoner. Reprinted by permission of the author.

Diane Wakoski: "From a Girl in a Mental Institution" from *Coins and Coffins*, Hawk's Well Press, 1982, copyright by Diane Wakoski. Reprinted by permission of the author.

Jeanne Murray Walker: "Seizure" from *Poetry*, reprinted in *Coming into History* by Jeanne Murray Walker, Cleveland State University Press, 1985. Reprinted by permission of the author.

Ronald Wallace: "After Being Paralyzed from the Neck down for Twenty Years, Mr. Wallace Gets a Chin-Operated Motorized Wheelchair" from *Plums, Stones, Kisses and Hooks*, University of Missouri Press, 1981, copyright by Ronald Wallace. Reprinted by permission of the author.

Belle Waring: "Baby Random" from *Refuge*, University of Pittsburgh Press, copyright 1990 by Belle Waring. Reprinted by permission of the publisher. "A Twenty-Four-Week Preemie, Change of Shift" from *Cape Discovery: The Provincetown Fine Arts Work Center Anthology*, Sheep Meadow Press, 1994. Reprinted by permission of the author and the publisher.

Michael Waters: "The Story of the Caul" from *Yale Review*, reprinted in *Anniversary of the Air*, Carnegie-Mellon University Press, 1985, copyright by Michael Waters. Reprinted by permission of the author.

Robert Watson: "At the Doctor's" from *Selected Poems*, Atheneum. Reprinted by permission of the author.

Theodore Weiss: "A Pair of Shoes" copyright 1994 by Theodore Weiss. Reprinted by permission of the author.

Thomas Whitbread: "Dying Body" from *Whomp and Moonshiver*,

# Index